Performance Pay as a Competitive Weapon

Performance Pay as a Competitive Weapon

A Compensation Policy Model for the 1990s

K. Richard Berlet
Douglas M. Cravens

John Wiley & Sons, Inc.

New York   Chichester   Brisbane   Toronto   Singapore

Library of Congress Cataloging-in-Publication Data
Berlet, K. Richard, 1946–
    Performance pay as a competitive weapon: A compensation policy model for the 1990s / by K. Richard Berlet and Douglas M. Cravens.
        p.   cm.
    Includes bibliographical reference and index.
    ISBN 0-471-52426-3 (cloth)
    1. Compensation management.   I. Cravens, Douglas M., 1947–   .
    II. Title.
    HF5549.5.C67B48   1991
    658.3'2--dc20   90-43501

Printed in the United States of America
91 92 10 9 8 7 6 5 4 3 2 1

No discipline can lengthen a man's arm. But it can lengthen his reach by hoisting him on the shoulders of his predecessors. Knowledge organized in a discipline does a good deal for the merely competent; it endows him with some effectiveness. It does more for the truly able; it endows him with excellence.

Peter Drucker

═══ Preface ═══

A black hole has existed since the early days of the business-strategy consultants, and it has swallowed all who have attempted to superimpose business analysis on the formulation of compensation policy. So at first glance, it might seem quixotic that a couple of veterans from this clash with the status quo should start a compensation consulting practice that is based on a business-analysis premise. But mounting frustration among many in the business world with the divergence of pay and performance, coupled with our own disappointment with the pretense of science and precision that veils our compensation consulting profession, seemed to spark the right chemistry for a fresh attack.

A lot is published on this subject. Unfortunately, though, the existing commentary brings to mind Victor Hugo's characterization of a discipline that "with its pretended depth . . . dissects effect without going back to the causes." Headlines in the press dwell on executives who rake in millions of dollars each year through cash and stock bonus programs; academics painstakingly carry out research to analyze and confirm what we already know—that pay and performance are largely uncorrelated; and experts administer an infinite array of surveys to validate any compensation arrangement a company might conceive. With this legacy, our principal aims in this book are to analyze the causes of the compensation discipline's stagnation, to lead the compensation policymakers beyond mindless imitation of their peers, and to embolden them, using a powerful compensation theory, to set their own course in uniting pay and performance.

We use the term *compensation theory* advisedly, knowing full well that skeptics may leap to the conclusion that the principles and methods discussed in this book are only theoretical. But rest assured, every concept described in the following pages has undergone the acid test of live application. Unlike many other management disciplines, compensation policy is encyclopedic in its cataloging of conventional practice, yet it lacks even a shadow of a theoretical framework. Consequently, as we set a new direction for compensation policy, an analytical framework that persistently challenges the discipline's fixation on conformity is a mandatory starting point.

Our fresh perspective on this staid subject comes from combining the aggressive style of our upstart consulting practice with thoughtful clients willing to redefine compensation policy boundaries in solving their companies' problems. In reflecting on our previous tenure as partners at a large human resources consulting firm, we realized that neither element of this admixture was in place: The values of the firm did not encourage us to take risks with long-standing client relationships; and for the most part, our clients were more interested in our firm's imprimatur than in the creativity of our product. So, now that we've spent five years in the incubator with our new company, it is time for us to thank all of those clients who helped to launch this business and who, with their persistent challenge of conventional wisdom, have forced an objective reexamination of every tenet of our practice.

As consultants writing an book heavily drawn from our personal experience with these clients, we had to choose how best to use this experience to illustrate our thoughts and ideas in action. By electing to disguise company identities, we may have relinquished the instant credibility and recognition that our more public clients might provide us. In return, however, we used the license of anonymity to sharpen our critique of client circumstances and to exploit their teaching value as we demonstrate intricate compensation concepts.

We could not conclude this preface without acknowledging the perseverance and dedication of Diane Kubitz in deciphering and rendering legible the endless drafts of this book. We also want to give particular thanks to Lowell S. Berlet, who never failed in his editorial trek through these pages to impose his template of precise language and disciplined logic. Finally, we are also indebted to Virginia H. Dimond for her tenacious critique of the concepts and insightful commentary on the entire manuscript.

K. Richard Berlet
Douglas M. Cravens

Triad Consultants, Inc.
Lincolnshire, Illinois
January 1991

══ Contents ══

Introduction   1

Chapter 1   Bedrock   11
   The Greening of the Executive Suite   12
   The Wheel of Compensation Policy   23

Chapter 2   Compensation Newspeak   37
   Word Currency   37
   On to the Gist   44

Chapter 3   The Pay Hierarchy Dilemma   45
   Stretching Base Salary   45
   Moving to a Higher Plane   56
   Living through Implementation: A Case Example   65

Chapter 4   Performance Units: Where the Buck Stops   71
   Prefab Performance Units   72
   The Inner Organization   76
   Forging a New Taxonomy   84

Chapter 5   Pay Risk: Impact beyond Equity   99
   The Research Illusion   101
   A License for Individual Initiative   103
   Job Evaluation's Third Dimension   106

**Chapter 6   Performance Measurement: In Search of
    Added Value**   119
   The Many Faces of Simplicity   120
   The Tale of the Tape   125

Sizing Up the Performance Measures   131
The Jagged Line to Strategic Performance   143
Added Value: A Road Less Traveled   144

Chapter 7 Cats, Dogs, Cows, and Compensation   **147**
Business-Strategy Paradigms   148
Models for the Middle   153
The Compensation Connection   156
Captive New-Venture Managers   163

Chapter 8 Incentive Engineering: Springloading the Message   **169**
Dissecting the Payout Curve   170
A Multigoal Incentive Structure with "Teeth"   176
The Power of Compound Incentives   181
A Payout Grid with Traffic Lights   185
Engineering without a Blueprint   187

Chapter 9 The Medium and the Message: Equity for the Right Reasons   **189**
Specious Reference Points   190
Equity or Not Equity   194
Stock Status   210

Chapter 10 Postscript   **203**

Appendix A Executive Pay Takes a Random Walk: Analysis of the *Business Week* Scoreboard   **205**

Appendix B A Précis of Long-Term Reward Systems   **209**

References   221
Index   223

Performance Pay as a Competitive Weapon

= Introduction =

"Pay for performance" is a tattered banner that corporate leaders passionately wave in advocating their compensation-management philosophy. Unfortunately, preoccupation with simplicity in communication and competitive industry practice all too often prevent the unfurling of these philosophical principles. During the past 30 years the tools available to help managers plan and measure the performance of their businesses have, primarily through the explosion in information sciences, attained a degree of sophistication that would have seemed surrealistic to the 1950s "organization man." Nevertheless, any careful analysis of modern-day compensation programs would fail to reveal a comparable advance in compensation technology.

In the absence of any discernible compensation *theory*, CEOs and technicians alike are forced to rely exclusively on existing *practice* and external peer comparisons for piecing together their compensation programs. They must copy the pay-for-performance structures, pay-risk levels, eligibility rules, and other components of similar companies, or perhaps make minor alterations to conventional practices using their own instincts as a guide. But using the new theory developed in this book, these policy planners can combine their instincts with an analytical framework to break the bonds of conventional practice and directly relate each component of a pay system to the nature and competitive position of their particular companies.

Reforming the Compensation Discipline

Management is recognizing the potential of compensation policy as a means to achieve competitive advantage in the marketplace; yet the practical implementation of this vision is limited by a compensation technology whose watchwords, "attract, retain, and motivate," hearken more to the era of the "organization man" than to the information age of the 1990s. In the last decade, much has been made of the ascendancy of human resources management in the corporate pecking order, and of the human resources manager's expanding contribution to a company's competitive strength. Many companies, however, are still entrenched in their view of the old-line personnel function, and the resident compensation experts have failed to argue compellingly for management's attention to the nuances of compensation policy formulation.

The primary intent of this book is to present a new set of rules for developing compensation policy and to demonstrate how nuances can affect individual and company performance at every level of the organization. Rather than serving up old wine in a new bottle, as is done in the overabundance of articles and research findings that appear in the current trade press, this book adopts a fresh pattern of analysis for fusing the disciplines of business strategy, organization, and compensation. It provides a diagnostic framework as well as prescriptions for formulating a business-analysis–based compensation strategy. The conventional building blocks of compensation policy—pay structure, mix, performance measures, and so forth—remain unaltered. However, in answering the following questions, this book illuminates with business reasoning and competitive strategy perspective many facets of these building blocks that have previously been shielded from the light of penetrating analysis:

- Should base salary or total compensation be used as the anchor for a company's pay hierarchy?
- Should management compensation hierarchies be separate from, or integrated with, sales and technical function hierarchies?
- What organizational parameters govern the amount of pay at risk for positions at various levels in the organization?
- How can incentive policy groups be used to break down provincialism embedded in organizational structure?
- How can performance measures be tested for their fit with a manager's sphere of authority and for their sensitivity to the manager's crucial decision trade-offs?
- How should the character of a business and its maturity influence the use of financial and nonfinancial performance measures? What mix of long- and short-term incentives is appropriate?
- When does stock work as a true incentive? When does it act primarily as a vehicle for executive capital accumulation?

In answering these questions, the book's prescriptions purposely stretch the conventional notions of pay for performance to their practical limits. And because of this aggressive tactic, readers can view the full spectrum of pay-for-performance issues, cafeteria style, and extract techniques and ideas that fit the current circumstances of their particular companies.

Adversaries of Change

First, it is necessary to examine in some detail the formidable adversaries to the introduction of any new compensation theory: entrenched technology, widespread cynicism, and the tax code diversion. Entrenched technology can be an obstacle to change in almost any discipline when established practice creates a comfort zone of familiarity and acceptability that preempts the consideration of new principles and ideas. On the other hand, cynicism by itself can be a stimulus for change. But in the compensation discipline, the root causes of this cynicism can be traced to a legacy of complacent policy management and specious dogma that is almost unshakable. Finally, the tax-favored treatment of certain forms of compensation has so preoccupied the policy planner's agenda for the past few years that the business rationale for incentives has been virtually obliterated.

Entrenched Technology

Peter Drucker and other business visionaries speak of work-force knowledge as the twenty-first century's bulwark of competitive strength, and global competition looms large as a force complicating performance measurement and management accountabilities. Current compensation technology, however, responds in monotone to these challenges by persisting in its simplistic focus on traditional goals—external competitiveness, internal equity, and communication simplicity—rather than redefining pay for performance as a vital competitive tool. To set a new course for policy formulation, this book must reexamine almost every tenet of prevailing compensation practice, including the notion of competitiveness and what it means for pricing an individual job in the labor market, and even the discipline's indelible watchwords of attract, retain, and motivate.

Base Salaries
The primal concern of internal equity has been addressed by a vast array of job evaluation systems that establish the hierarchy of jobs in an or-

ganization. In addition, by matching the pay levels of selected positions to data on the same positions in peer companies, the external competitiveness of the base-salary structure can also be appraised. Though these guideposts remain relevant, application of the job evaluation systems has tended to become a purely technical, even mechanical exercise. Thus, the finer points of organization design and changing corporate values are glossed over without the reexamination of several critical questions:

- Are the same labor market data relevant for all functions and positions in the organization?
- Should all positions be targeted at the same level relative to the competitive range?
- What job evaluation methodology fits the company's personality and management style?
- Can a single set of factors adequately measure job values throughout the company?
- Do salary grade steps adequately match all career paths in the company, or do some functions have special requirements?

Incentives

The approach to incentive plan design, like that to salary management, has tended to seek the lowest common denominator of mechanical simplicity. Any incentive arrangement that requires more than a single phrase or sentence to describe its payout formula is often viewed as overly complex and vague. With this mind-set, policymakers create incentive plans that tend to be structurally sound but rely on generic performance measures which only distally relate to the company's business or strategy and nominally influence management behavior.

The portion of compensation that is placed "at risk" through incentive programs has almost always been reduced to a study in competitive research. For each reporting level that is slated to receive a bonus, the policy planners review the proportions of base salary and bonus in competitive companies, or general industry, to establish a "competitive" mix policy in their own company. This procedure is followed religiously, even though the research, regardless of its scope, does not capture the important variations in mix that accompany differences in leadership style, organization structure, and competitive positioning.

This book does not promote complexity in base salary or incentive policy for the sake of complexity; nor does it recommend simplicity for simplicity's sake, thereby ignoring the manifold components that make up performance. Its purpose is to provide the policy planner with a font of useful guidelines and analytical methods with which to challenge the prevailing technology and, even when an element of this technology has been adopted, to support its usage with a sound *business* rationale independent of conventionality.

Cloud of Cynicism

At the same time that simplicity and familiarity became the cornerstones of compensation policy in the 1970s and 1980s, the failure of companies' performances to keep pace with advances in management pay levels has bred public cynicism toward the "pay-for-performance" dictum. Though an undercurrent of this dissent is present in the business community throughout the year, public outcry reaches a crescendo with the annual publication in the business press of executive pay levels.

Among these scorecards of executive pay, the version published in *Business Week* offers a useful tool for reviewing trends over an extended period. We tracked the pay-for-performance record of 163 companies that are common to the three most recent publications (1987, 1988, 1989) in this series and found (after some data reorganization) the first source of cynicism: a relationship between executive pay and company financial performance that is virtually random (see Appendix A for detailed results of our analysis).

A similar but more extensive commentary on this lack of correlation appears in the 1987 *Business Week* Scoreboard cover story, which cited a study by professors Michael C. Jensen and Kevin J. Murphy at the University of Rochester that examined the relationship between pay and performance. After looking at nearly 2,000 executives in 1,200 companies, the professors statistically rejected the pay-for-performance hypothesis and concluded that "executives tend to be overpaid for bad performance and underpaid for good performance." In light of this and kindred forms of evidence, it is understandable that investors and the general public are becoming more strident in their plea for management's "value added."

Enter the ubiquitous consultants. Searching for a response to this escalating protest, companies have come to rely heavily on consultants for the design and validation of their compensation programs. Over time, the source of preference for these specialists has shifted from the major strategy and organization consulting firms to professional firms grounded in the technical human resources management disciplines (for example, benefits, insurance, personnel administration, salary management, actuarial services). This shift from a business policy to a technical focus leads us to the second source of cynicism: Compensation specialists and their client counterparts have progressively narrowed the scope of compensation policy and have disregarded its linkage to the company's broader business policy and strategy concerns.

Compounding this ever-narrowing view is the conflict of interest inherent in the consultants' pay level recommendations for the same managers who hire them. Though the solution to this conflict of interest is readily apparent—the insertion of the board compensation committee as the consultant's client—most boards take a cheap seat in the bleachers when pay levels are set. When confronted with the prospect of pay more strictly tied to performance uncertainties, they rationalize their invertebrate posture with concerns for executive retention that ostensibly outweigh their concerns for company performance, yielding yet another source of cynicism. A recent *Fortune* magazine article quoted Pfizer CEO Edmund Pratt, Jr. (who sits on several compensation committees) as saying, "You just can't keep your guys if you allow a lot of swing in pay. People can't hire that way, and boards don't let it happen." The public therefore is viewing with healthy skepticism the tumesence of pay in the absence of an apparent business rationale.

The waning objectivity of compensation policymakers is exacerbated by the final source of cynicism: the classic risk-avoidance bias of the human resources function. In these days of the Equal Employment Opportunity Commission and legislated employment rights, and with the ongoing complexities of labor relations, it is a legitimate and necessary mission of human resources management to walk a fine line between the interests of the company and those of individual employees. Unfortunately, this mission's halo too often extends to compensation policy as well, and programs are designed that simply mimic unassailable industry norms. Certainly this tactic protects the program designer from the quicksand of corporate politics and personal opinion, but it rarely leads to a close examination of what will truly benefit the business. What's more, this lack of business analysis further isolates the human resources function from the inner sanctum of strategic policy.

To earn their way into this select group, human resources professionals must take intellectual risks and speak out forcefully and imaginatively on compensation policy issues from a podium firmly anchored in the company's business strategy. The purpose of this book, therefore, is to prescribe for all policy planners (human resources professionals and their board compensation committee counterparts) a new theory that relates each element of compensation policy to the characteristics of a company—its organization structure, competitive position, and leadership style. To use these principles and methods, however, compensation specialists can no longer rely solely on technical compensation skills and knowledge of the IRS code. First and foremost, they must become adept business analysts acutely mindful of their company's competitive strategy and performance mandates. In like manner, board members can no longer rubber-stamp compensation policy with a single-minded focus on executive retention. Instead they must critically examine the business purpose and logic of any payout formula. Armed with this powerful compensation theory and a new bridge to the board compensation committee, policy planners can then take the lead in diffusing the cloud of cynicism that hangs over the performance-pay discipline.

The Tax Code Diversion

The Tax Reform Act of 1986 eliminated, at least temporarily, a distraction for compensation policymakers. With the disbanding of the capital gains tax treatment, the design focus of many compensation programs shifted from "tax effectiveness" techniques to cash delivery. In the prereform era, planners made extensive use of cash compensation alternatives, such as stock grants and options in various forms, to take advantage of tax code treatments favorable to both the executives and the company. After the reform, however, stock as a payment medium could no longer remain a preference of unquestioned validity. In addition, the volatility of stock prices in the markets of the 1980s, heightened by the so-called merger mania and leveraged buyout binges, has further eroded the attractiveness of company stock as an incentive medium.

Even if the markets stabilize and the Bush administration is successful in reinstating the tax preference for capital gains, the compensation planner should remain cautious in using stock in incentive pay plans. The traditional justification that these plans serve as long-term incentives closely tied to shareholder interests, when in fact they have been adopted primarily for their tax effectiveness, is a hollow argument in the face of more stringent scrutiny of management's value added.

Though stock-based compensation can act, in special circumstances, as an incentive to influence management behavior, the sagacious planner will critically examine all stock programs introduced under the "incentive" banner and openly acknowledge when the primary intent of a grant or option is acutally capital accumulation. Thus, by clearly separating these classes of stock-based compensation, policy planners can help to dissipate the cloud of cynicism by distinguishing between pure incentive pay (ostensibly related to performance) and other forms of pay more closely tied to retirement income and perquisites.

Using This Book

This book is written to create a new language of compensation policy that will open the lines of communication between senior executives and human resources professionals and, in turn, elevate incentive compensation to the plateau of a fundamental strategic concern. By focusing on this broad business purpose, technicians, compensation researchers, and administrators of compensation policy are led through a new analytical process that is fraught with political risks and uncertain outcomes. In keeping with this purpose, practitioners looking for a compendium of academic viewpoints and research esoterica will find instead case examples and real-life prescriptions.

Because the subjects of sales force compensation and productivity incentives for the nonexempt work force are extensive topics unto themselves, we will not address them, except in passing. This book zeroes in on middle- and senior-management compensation issues and borrows liberally from the productivity and sales compensation principles (where pay for performance has a rich and respected legacy) to augment the existing practices of management compensation. The concepts of this book may also be applied to nonmanagerial, exempt positions (those typically lost between the cracks of incentive eligibility criteria) by companies particularly adept at performance measurement and organization analysis.

The book follows a progression, from the initial "Bedrock" chapter that sets up a conceptual model enumerating and defining each of the major components of compensation policy, through chapters on the relationship between organization design and compensation structure, and then to a series of chapters on incentive compensation and its relationship to business strategy. The final chapter explores the use and misuse of stock programs, centering on the place of stock in the incentive program portfolio as a counterbalancing incentive to annual bonus programs; little attention is given to the popularity of stock programs as a capital-accumulation vehicle.

The materials presented in this book can be used in several different ways. CEOs and senior executives can dip into a particular chapter for conceptual stimulus in examining current or proposed compensation policies in the context of their company's strategy. Human resources and compensation professionals can also draw on the book in various ways:

1. It can be used as a reference guide, similar to the use described for a CEO.
2. It can be used as a step-by-step manual for defining and evaluating compensation policy alternatives: The first part of the book examines the principles of designing and administering a compensation hierarchy, then addresses the compensation mix questions and prescribes a method of sorting the organization into policy groupings; next, the book addresses the crucial concern of selecting the incentive program performance criteria that are the essential distillates of the company's strategy; finally, the book provides new ideas for operationally linking compensation components and fortifying the performance management architecture.
3. Human resources and compensation professionals can also use this book as a source of case examples that illuminate the organization and management issues that must be addressed during the design and implementation of a new program. The introduction of any significant change in compensation policy will inevitably give rise to pockets of dissent and organizational disruption. In keeping with the guiding vision of this book—to integrate compensation policy with organization and business strategy considerations— case examples are used extensively to illustrate how executives in diverse businesses have used the suggested approaches to strengthen their performance management discipline while reconciling the crosscurrents of dissent among their key managers.

To help the reader distinguish this book's new concepts from conventional wisdom, it is desirable that he or she be familiar with most direct compensation terminology and with the professional literature on competitive strategy and management theory. Preexisting convictions about compensation policy, though not essential, will no doubt heighten sensitivity to the subtleties and nuances embodied in our approach. On the other hand, without an open mind and the patience to plumb the depths of the concepts, the reader may be tempted to gloss over them in search of "answers." But before succumbing to this temptation, one should keep in mind that the purpose of this book is to help compensation planners formulate their *own* answers using a policy framework that compounds the effect of subtle changes and truly sets a new course for linking pay to performance.

1

Bedrock

Most companies today maintain that at least some element of their employees' pay is tied to "performance," but the frustration and wry commentary of managers, investment analysts, and the business press surrounding "pay for performance" indicate that the eroding credibility of these programs encroaches on other realms of business policy. Because public companies, in particular, go to great lengths to place executive compensation decisions in the hands of their outside directors, it is natural to assume that flaws in these decisions portend a more general management malaise. Recent reports that General Motors, United Airlines, and other prominent companies have been under fire from their institutional investors on the details of the companies' management pay systems and performance standards suggest that this malaise has moved the investing community beyond words and into action.

Arguably, the critics are correct when they assume that business policy decisions should have a spillover effect on any pay-for-performance program. When boards discuss organization restructuring, changes in leadership, or competitive strategies, it follows that compensation arrangements should be adjusted to reflect modified performance priorities and accountabilities. In reality, however, the central board-level question for most executive pay packages is *How much?*—not *How?*, or *For What?* Consequently, pay decisions are the product of an administrative system theme rather than one of broad business policy that couples incentive pay with business strategy.

To rescue pay for performance from its credibility tailspin, board compensation committees must raise compensation policy from its administrative stature to that of a leading force in communicating the company's values. Toward this end, compensation should take a seat alongside the CEO in setting the management tone and leadership style of the organization. And, whereas tone and style transcend organization structure and hierarchy, compensation systems must also extend beyond these conventional boundaries and align themselves with performance boundaries that are defined by the authority and decision structure of the company.

To reflect this change in perspective, a new term, *achievement pay*, supplants the old "pay-for-performance" moniker in both name and spirit. This change in nomenclature is more than just literary gimmickry; it is expressly intended to convey a sharpened focus on management's value added—or what management does that makes a difference to the company. In spirit, compensation policy will now be concerned as much with competitive strategy and its execution—how a result is achieved—as with the actual financial results that have been the familiar touchstones of today's systems.

The Greening of the Executive Suite

Some claim that it all started in 1918, when General Motors' pioneering CEO, Alfred Sloan, introduced a bonus program that paid managers extra cash compensation contingent on company earnings. Though this program helped link a manager's pay to the company's overall performance, its highly discretionary nature left the bonus amounts and the basis for individual payments an untold mystery. For the most senior managers at GM, this program probably had a real influence on their decision-making behavior because, as part of the company's policy inner sanctum, they could witness firsthand the impact of their actions. The original version of this plan excluded those managers who held positions deeper in the organization, where policy execution, rather than policy formulation, occurs. Perhaps Sloan felt that at the middle and lower levels of the organization, the sense of ownership in the company's directional policies was too weak for his bonus plan to have an impact on management behavior. Nevertheless, imitating GM's profit-sharing bonus programs, many companies today have extended participation in their plans to middle-management levels well down the organizational ladder.

The Sloan Plan's Life Cycle

Through the years, as the Sloan—or "Christmas turkey"—type of bonus plan was popularized, it became tagged with the "incentive" label and was widely adopted as a universal compensation concept. But when such programs are placed in the arena of today's large corporations with their complex and bureaucratic organization structures, there are manifold reasons to question their real incentive value. Undaunted, countless CEOs still stand up and moralistically proclaim that *all* employees *should* feel a genuine sense of ownership and be able to localize their personal impact on a company's welfare. Adapting these programs to their special environments, compensation policymakers have developed several mechanical or systems refinements.

Publication of Bonus Formula

To create more of a before-the-fact incentive orientation to the programs, the relationship between the amount of bonus paid and the company's actual performance is predefined. In the simplest formulas, a portion of earnings is set aside for distribution to the employees, contingent on the company's achieving a minimum threshold of earnings. Except for the participation and distribution limitations of today's tax-qualified profit-sharing retirement plans, these rudimentary bonus pools operate at a similar level of abstraction and usually act as only passive influences on employee behavior.

The executive bonus program at CBS, in place for nearly 50 years, offers a classic example of bonus program arcanum. It sets aside 4 percent of after-tax profits as a pool in which the executives can share. Over time, as CBS's earnings have grown to more than $1 billion, the pool has risen to flood proportions—$40 million. Analysis of this plan as stated in the proxy leaves untold just how large the shareholder's liability really is or what factors will actually determine how much is paid to executives.

Broadened Participation

Ironically, when more and more managers become eligible to participate in the programs, an explicit communication of organizational hierarchy is necessary and, in turn, an employee "caste" system is created. This refinement, and its attendant layering of the organization, evolved gradually, as management defined criteria that qualified employees for participation in the program. Typically, the boundaries of participation groups are delineated by base salary or salary grade thresholds; higher bonus opportunities are granted to positions near the top of this hierarchy, regardless of their accountabilities. Though this "innovation" arrived on the heels of Sloan's original concept, the base salary threshold approach to defining incentive policy groups has enjoyed little enrichment or constructive scrutiny in the intervening years.

Diversification of Performance Measures

To extend management accountability beyond the income statement and into the arcane world of the balance sheet, a repertoire of more sophisticated financial ratios is required. Companies recognized that, just because earnings exceed the threshold prescribed to activate these broad-based incentive programs, the full performance story is not always told. Additionally, the broadening participation and attendant cost of these programs typically exacerbates management's discontent with a single threshold.

Although senior management has the perspective to easily grasp the trade-offs between growth and earnings and the attendant asset management implications, these concerns are not as comprehensible for managers at lower levels in the organization. Sensing that lower-level managers need unambiguous directives, companies have expanded the performance criteria of these incentive plans so that the accurate communication of performance priorities is not left to chance.

Unfortunately, one of the best examples in U.S. industry of a failure to make this transition occurred in the steel industry, where a consistent and exclusive focus on short-term earnings, reinforced through the message of executive compensation programs, drove management to ignore the threat of technological change. Similarly, an incentive program for the officers of Continental Illinois Bank that focused exclusively on loan volume played no small part in this bank's highly visible misfortunes in the early 1980s.

Deferral of Payments

To allow executives to be taxed at lower rates during their retirement years on a portion of their annual earnings, special deferral programs have been created. These programs probably gained popularity as executives' pay levels began to exceed their annual economic need. In an accommodating manner, the IRS has allowed executives to delay the constructive receipt of profit-sharing or bonus distributions (i.e., actual receipt of the money for personal use) until retirement and thereby avoid an immediate tax liability. Though these deferred payments are sometimes tied to meaningful performance criteria, the absence of "cash in-hand" tends to muffle the communication of performance priorities and, in turn, dilute the incentive value of the programs.

Discretionary Awards

To provide a one-time recognition bonus payment to individuals who make an extraordinary contribution to the company, special lump-sum bonus pools have been provided to managers for allocation to subordinates. Clearly, these awards can be significant morale boosters. But they should be recognized as just an updated version of the original Sloan plan by virtue of their discretionary nature and their obscure link to individual performance standards.

On the upside, recipients of these awards are no doubt delighted with their newfound wealth, even though they are usually unsure of how the bonus is connected to their personal performance. On the downside, the managers who, for whatever reasons, do not receive awards may very likely perceive that they have been singled out for punitive treatment. Consequently, these discretionary awards act principally as attitude amplifiers instead of directional incentives, and over time, their effect can compound and give a manipulative tone to management's handling of all employees.

Smaller, private companies are the predominant users of discretionary awards today, and without question, these programs work best when the employees implicitly trust top management and believe in the fairness of the discriminatory judgments made about individual performers. Small-company owners find, however, that as their companies grow and senior management's relationship with the employees becomes more distant, the credibility of these discretionary incentive programs is eroded. A recent study by Carnegie-Mellon's Robert Kelley suggests that employee trust is difficult to come by and should not be taken for granted. In his survey of 400 managers, fully one-third revealed that they distrust their own bosses, and 55 percent question top management's forthrightness.

Diversification of Compensation Media

Purportedly, stock-based programs have been used to tie executives' interests to those of the shareholders, to lengthen the time horizon of an incentive program, and, "incidentally," to reap the benefits of capital-gains tax preferences. Just as management found that a single performance measure failed to capture the full range of *annual* managerial achievement, they also discovered that even multiple performance measures did not adequately accommodate the extended planning horizon for their businesses.

Searching for a vehicle to meet this longer-term incentive need, companies naturally gravitated to common stock and its professed record of tracking the long view of a business's intrinsic value. Maybe it was only coincidental that stock, up until recently, also happened to possess an attractive tax preference status, but it is hard today to find a *Fortune* 1,000 company that does not have some form of stock-based compensation for its senior executives.

Notwithstanding this level of acceptance, stock-based plans should still meet stringent tests to qualify as true incentives, since the relationship between manager performance and stock price is illusive and subject to myriad intervening variables. William Neikirk summed up his view on the folly of using stock price in the 1980s as a mirror of manager performance in an editorial in the *Chicago Tribune* when he wrote, "Stock prices are directly related to the ease by which debt can be accumulated by potential bidders for takeover targets." Even as merger mania slows and the raw fundamentals of interest and earnings once again influence the market, the volatility induced by program trading and its amplification of corporate "newscasts" will continue to frustrate any attempt at correlating manager performance and stock price.

The culmination of all these refinements is a compensation discipline that today speaks of executive pay packages as if, having deposited the correct change, one can pluck them from a vending machine. One might even be tempted to conclude, after reviewing all of the upgrades to Sloan's original idea discussed thus far, that great strides have been taken toward the ideal of "true" achievement pay and that cloning the compensation systems used by successful companies in an industry is a practical, and even strategic, course of action.

A closer look reveals that most of these advances in compensation "technology" have been in the mechanics, rather than the art, of linking pay to performance and are rooted in technique rather than business analysis. The variations in plan components, from participation criteria to payout media, for annual and long-term incentive programs, are shown in Figure 1.1. In Figures 1.2 and 1.3, ingredients from this menu are selected and combined to create "boilerplate" incentive plans that are representative of the current-day standard fare (except for their attendant legal wrappers).

Even as this book just begins to scratch the surface of a more exact achievement pay concept, careful probing of this menu and the boilerplate plans should raise more questions for the reader than it answers. In much the same way that a master chef strives for a balance of flavors and textures in combining various courses in a gourmet meal, the compensation planner must also blend ingredients that complement and support a business strategy. A recipe to guide the matching of components in each cell of Figure 1.1 with a business strategy remains elusive, however; and in the absence of this conjunctive rationale, the compensation planner searches for the "perfect" performance measure, the ideal structural mechanism, or another creative tax loophole as a false step toward elevating the art of achievement pay to its next plateau. Our premise, however, is that compensation policy should occupy a seat alongside the CEO in setting the company's tone and leadership style. The compensation planner's futile search must therefore be replaced by an improved analytical process that more precisely mates the wide variety of compensation elements, already well defined, to the strategic performance units embedded in the company's organization.

Changing Ownership Structure

The "Christmas turkey" incentive model works well, as noted earlier, where an owner is openly accessible and actively involved with all the incentive participants when important decisions are made. In the years since the inception of this model, however, corporate ownership has become institutionalized and has lost the organic character that owner-managers could provide. Big investors such as pension funds, insurance companies, and mutual funds now concentrate up to 3 percent of their assets in a single company's stock. In fact, according to the Securities Industry Association, these institutional investors own 43 percent of the public stock of U.S. companies, and institutional trading (including Wall Street firms trading for their own account) totals just under 80 percent of the New York Stock Exchange volume. Together with the recent binge of debt financing used to leverage mergers and buyouts, banks and institutional investors are now a pervasive influence on the decision making of corporate management. In this more bureaucratic structure, unhealthy pay strategies have emerged in the 1980s.

Plan Components	Selections for Annual Plans
Participant cutoffs	Top management Sr. line/staff Middle management
Target bonus:	
Top management	40% to 60%
Sr. line/staff	35% to 50%
Middle management	15% to 30%
Performance criteria: Top management Sr. line/staff Middle management	Company financial (ROE, EPS, Earnings, EPS growth) Combination of company financial and individual accountability
Payout structure	Range above and below objective (i.e., 85% to 130% of objective) No payment below objective; accelerated payouts above objective
Payout media	Cash Stock options ⎱ used Restricted stock grants ⎰ infrequently

Figure 1.1 Executive Incentive Plans: Menu of Typical Ingredients

Selections for Long-Term Plans
Top management Sr. line/staff
‑ 30% to 100% annualized ‑ 20% to 60% annualized ‑ (usually not applicable)
Company financial (ROE, EPS, Earnings, EPS   growth) Share price appreciation

Range above and below objective based on cumulative
  performance
Range above and below objective based on performance at end
  of plan cycle
Appreciation in share price × number of shares, phantom shares,
  or performance units

Cash Stock options Stock Combination of cash and stock

1. *Objectives*
    a. Provide a competitive total pay package for the attraction and retention of qualified managers
    b. Enhance management communication by focusing attention on profit performance management
    c. Control fixed salary costs
2. *Participation*
    Eligibility will be at the discretion of the compensation committee, but limited to managers who can significantly influence the company's financial performance:

Group	Description
A	Holding company senior vice president
B	Holding company vice president or subsidiary president
C	Subsidiary vice presidents

3. *Performance Measures*
    Each year's pretax net income targets as established by the profit plan
4. *Potential Awards*
    If the planned objective threshold or a higher performance is achieved, a pool of performance awards will be funded:

	Incentive Payout as a Percentage of Base Salary		
	Performance Level		
Group	85%	100%	125%
A	20%	40%	60%
B	15	30	50
C	8	15	30

5. *Plan Administration*
    The compensation committee of the board shall be vested with the authority to administer the plan.

Figure 1.2   Boilerplate Annual Executive Incentive Plan

Short-Term Focus

The complaints that management attention centers on short-term results (despite the diversification of compensation media and performance measures mentioned previously), and that priorities for long-term growth and profit improvement are largely ignored, are widespread and recurrent. Nevertheless, a market led by institutional ownership continues to react impulsively to quarterly earnings reports; companies rationalize their borrowing against future cash flows to maintain dividend payouts; a prospective change in ownership almost always evokes a run-up in stock price, though the economic underpinnings of the run-up are frequently

1. *Participation*
   Participation in the plan will be limited to the following:
   a. Chairman of the board
   b. President
   c. Division managers (3)

2. *Plan Cycle*
   Plan cycles are three years in length with a new cycle starting each year. Thus, the first potential awards under the plan will be in three years, with potential awards paying every year thereafter.

3. *Performance Measures*
   The criteria for measuring performance is return on stockholder's equity (ROE). ROE is measured in terms of the average annual ROE over the three-year performance period, based on stockholder's equity at the beginning of each year.

4. *Potential Awards*
   The award will be based on the actual ROE over the performance period according to the following schedule:

Company ROE 1990—1992	Individual Performance Award as a Percentage of Base Salary
20%	20%
22	35
24 (target)	60
25	70
26	80

5. *Determination and Form of Award*
   The award will be based on each participant's average annual base salary over the three-year performance period. Payment of awards will be made in 66⅔% cash and 33⅓% common stock at book value.

Figure 1.3   Boilerplate Long-Term Executive Incentive Plan

illusive; and investor queries into company strategies, dominated by a retirement investment mentality, focus on next quarter's management initiatives and earnings projections.

Profit-Sharing Mind-set

The gilded age of the 1980s saw a burgeoning of uncapped pay formulas for top executives that were based on a percentage of profits that exceeded a certain threshold. One can only infer from these plans that the investor is saying, "As long as I get mine, then the executives are entitled to their share, in some direct proportion." A much-publicized example of this mind-set is the pay package designed for Michael D. Eisner, chairman of Walt Disney Company. Mr. Eisner's formula is quite simple: A threshold of 9 percent return on shareholders' equity is set as the floor for any incentive payment (this floor increases to 11 percent in 1991); Mr. Eisner receives 2 cents on each dollar earned in excess of this 9 percent threshold. In 1989, this profit-sharing scheme yielded a payment of nearly $10 million (exclusive of any stock options). In 1988, the payment was $6.8 million. Recent history is filled with other examples of extraordinary payments made to executives—extraordinary because of their sheer magnitude (Paul Fireman of Reebok receives 5 percent of the amount by which pretax earnings exceed $20 million; in 1989 his bonus was $14.2 million and has averaged $13.6 million a year over the past four years) or because of their mismatch with the company's welfare (the entire senior management corps of GM).

Looking closely at these pay schemes reveals that their impact on a company's welfare and achievement pay infrastructure can be debilitating on at least two fronts. First, from a purely financial perspective, making very large amounts of compensation contingent on a single dimension of performance invites manipulation of business policy in a manner that sacrifices all other concerns and interests for the one lucrative objective. Though, this is, we hope, not a revelatory observation, boards of directors responsible for authorizing these pay plans continue to whistle past the graveyard. Psychoanalysis of this syndrome is not within the scope of this book, but acknowledgment of the absurdity of paying Olympian incentives over a threshold that does not even cover a firm's cost of capital (e.g., Disney) is the first step toward a true achievement-pay system.

The second front of attack is on the organization itself and the skewed relationship between top management and the work force. As the compensation gulf between the lowest-level employee and the CEO widens and creates a new class of industrial superstars, indifference, or even animosity, can permeate the organization. This situation is not too unlike the one baseball team owners faced in the early 1940s, when they lost control of the payroll costs of their superstars. The owners could only stand by and watch as the players gained nationwide access to the public through the electronic media (particularly television) and created their independent public image.

Though it has taken quite a few years for more mundane business personalities to realize the potential of media hype, it became a reality in the 1980s with the lionization of Lee Iacocca. *In Search of Excellence*; the *People Magazine* style of *Forbes*, *Fortune*, and *Business Week*; and the broad media coverage of executive pay levels have all tended to push board compensation committees into a "the-sky's-the-limit" pay strategy. What has been forgotten through all this hype, though, is that corporate executives play on teams of 2,000, 5,000, and 30,000 players and that the highly paid executives are, for the most part, neither founders of the company nor substantial investors in it.

A few U.S. companies have sensed the pitfalls of superstar pay packages and have a stated policy of maintaining a fixed ratio between the compensation of the lowest-level personnel and that of the CEO. Ben & Jerry's gourmet ice cream company, for example, has limited the founders' compensation to a level that does not exceed a 5 to 1 ratio with the lowest-paid employee. In Japan and the United Kingdom, informal national industrial policy sets guidelines that place a practical ceiling on this gap. Most U.S. companies, on the other hand, dismiss this consideration as irrelevant. In so doing, they must certainly close their eyes to the distorting effect that the exorbitant pay levels of top executives, benefiting from uncapped "profit-sharing" incentive arrangements, have on the scale of human worth in their organizations. Though these profit-sharing formulas are appealingly simple, their insidious effect, though not always observed within the time horizon of the institutional investor, is inescapable.

Copycat Syndrome

Probably the single most important contributor to the current status of pay-for-performance systems is that top management and board compensation committees are fearful of deviating from established compensation patterns. Bluntly stated, these policymakers are addicted to conformity. As more is written about individual cases of the extreme, and even outrageous, compensation practices driven by simple "profit-sharing" formulas, the addiction is nourished, and the practices become the norm for the business community. In this way, a vicious circle of media hype, stoking an audience hungry for spoon-fed truths, creates an upward spiral of untethered executive pay levels. And where common sense leads management to look to the competitive marketplace for collective wisdom and guidance on compensation policy, reversion to a common sense closer to home may be the only fiscally responsible alternative to the "hyperpay" bandwagon.

The Wheel of Compensation Policy

The realm of compensation policy includes six primary components: organization, risk, medium, mechanics, timing, and performance. The contemporary approach to formulating compensation policy places organization structure at the focal point and manipulates the remaining components to protect the organization's hierarchy. Occasionally, however, the focal point has shifted to one of the other components in concert with management's priorities. One of the components is usually dominant and forms the "hub" of the policy wheel; the other five components take subordinate "spoke" roles in shaping policy (Figure 1.4).

To set the stage for a policy prescription that unfolds throughout the remaining chapters, in which performance is placed at the hub, it is necessary to examine the organization and management ramifications of centering policy on any one of the other components.

Organization Structure

The formal "chain of command," whether built on a functional, business-unit, geographical, or other premise, is a convenient graphic representation of an organization's accountabilities. Compensation planners usually assume that strategic impact and influence on key decisions is layered, in military fashion, like the organization's graphic depiction, and they have traditionally accepted this horizontal layering of an organization

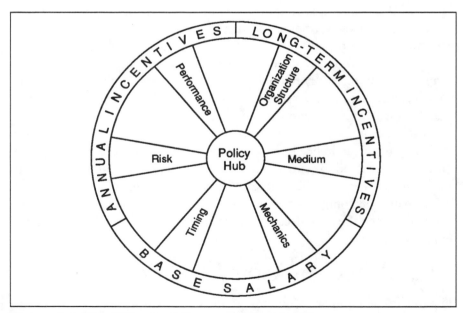

Figure 1.4 The Wheel of Compensation Policy

as the unassailable foundation for the development of a compensation strategy.

Starting at the top of the organization, lines segregating the successive reporting levels are used as the boundaries for selecting and matching various compensation components (see Figure 1.1). However, compensation planners should be cautious when relying on an organization's structure as a substrate for the application of pay systems. A literal interpretation of the organization structure will suggest that, in all cases, lower reporting level positions have less impact on results than positions in any function at a higher reporting level. When line positions are compared to high-level staff positions, the flaws in this horizontal segmentation may become painfully apparent. In a consumer products company, for example, this might mean that the corporate controller is strategically positioned alongside, or at a higher level than, the manager of the company's major product line.

Though "reorganization" is not a prerequisite for the effective operation of all new compensation programs, thorough testing of an organization's accountability structure and its fit with the company's strategy is an essential step. Organization development models consistently identify at least four major variables that must be considered to respond to a company's strategy. These variables usually include cultural, resource, systems, and structural dimensions. The theme common to most of these models is the interdependency of the organization variables. One clear message of the model illustrated in Figure 1.5(a) is that structure and reward systems are interactive. By implication, then, if one changes the structure of an organization, modification in the reward systems may be required. Also, according to the theory of this and other organization development models, an organizational problem may be resolved by use of a mixture of variables. As Figure 1.5(b) indicates, for example, information systems may create critical links in an organization's decision-making processes that could also be achieved through realignment of the organization structure. With this integrated view of organization development, management's prerogative, then, is to fit the variables together in a manner that is deemed optimal to the execution of its business strategy.

Despite the theory of these models, when management embarks on a reorganization course, it is usually with an exclusive concentration on the fit between structure and competitive strategy. Though this focus is sometimes management's last resort after the avenues employing the other

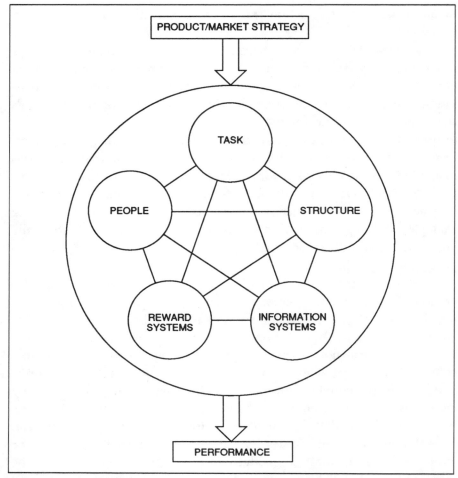

Figure 1.5(a) Organization Development Model

variables have been explored, it is more frequently the first course of action. Structural change tends to create a sense of dynamism that is comforting to management, particularly in tough times, and, unfortunately, manipulation of the other organizational variables is perceived as less majestic.

So, for the compensation planner who relies on the horizontal layering of an organization as the template for pay policies, there is a high risk that cultural, resource, management system, or even structural barriers to the success of a compensation program may be lurking just below the surface. Alternatively, if the planner's perspective permits a position tax-

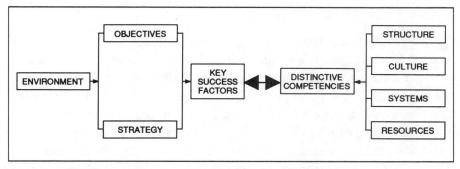

Figure 1.5(b) Organization Development Model

onomy that transcends organization structure, the planner can identify opportunities to bolster weaknesses in the organization by using the compensation system to highlight the indispensable relationships of key positions and their performance imperatives. Plotting jagged lines across functions and chains of command in this manner allows the compensation planner to encompass the full scope of an important business mission in an achievement-pay framework.

As a case in point, a large pharmaceutical company spent several years developing and commercially launching a new drug. In this long and arduous process, numerous functions across the organization (government affairs, research and development, medical affairs, marketing and sales, and product management) came together to define and execute portions of the product strategy. Each member of the development team was granted two distinct levels of authority: As discipline specialists on the project team, they had far-reaching decision authority that directly influenced the product strategy (and that might equate to the authority of company officers); within their "home" organizational segments, however, they followed a stricter regimen of authority that more closely mirrored the career steps of their discipline. Therefore, the formal structure of this company was at best only a starting point when it came to defining compensation policy groupings. To counterbalance the parochial interests and values of the home disciplines, the company needed a compensation system that would unify the project team and remove the company's formal organization structure from the hub of the compensation policy wheel. Accordingly, the corporate restrictions on incentive participation and the mix of base-salary and bonus components had to be set aside in favor of a new plan that incorporated launch milestone awards and introductory sales results.

Risk

Compensation risk is the portion of pay that an employee cannot reliably predict. For example, if a bonus plan is to pay 30 percent of base salary at target performance (i.e., achievement of 100 percent of objectives), and a bonus of less than 20 percent has not been paid in the last 10 years, then the at-risk portion of pay is really 10 percent, and not 30 percent. Risk, therefore, can be defined only in the context of a practical performance range that clearly delimits the minimum acceptable threshold of performance and the maximum practical level, above which only windfalls, or major external events, explain the results.

Sales forces provide a classic model of compensation risk at the hub of the policy wheel. In many industries (e.g., printing, distribution, advertising) it is common practice to pay the salespeople by means of a commission arrangement whereby each incremental dollar of revenue results in an incremental incentive payment. With this direct correlation between sales and compensation, management is assured that the ratio between sales costs and revenues will remain constant. Though management's defense of this type of compensation arrangement typically rests on the ability of commissions to roust the salesperson out of bed each morning, management rarely claims that a commission plan is able to point the sales force toward specific priorities.

Thus, those who cling steadfastly to this type of incentive compensation and even augment simple formulas with special premiums to create a directional thrust are at heart primarily attracted to the form—financial leverage—rather than the substance—management and direction—of an incentive program. With the sales force as a backdrop, many companies have adopted total company versions of the commission incentive structure, namely, profit-sharing plans tied to financial thresholds. In these types of plans, the amount paid to the work force directly tracks with the company's ability to afford additional payments.

A leading paper company provides a useful example of the confusion created when these profit-sharing plans become institutionalized. At the onset, this company adopted an elegantly uncomplicated structure for sharing profits with the entire work force that regularly added a 12 percent to 18 percent year-end bonus to each employee's salary. During the early years of this program, a cost-control culture permeated the organization and offered consistently high margins in an otherwise price-driven industry. By reinvesting these profits in manufacturing technology and capacity, the company was able to sustain its competitive advantage, and its gain-sharing plan, for many years.

However, the bonus plan that began as a clearly communicated add-on to competitive salaries evolved into a cacophony of mixed messages. Even in the executive suite, the chairman and the vice president of human resources could no longer agree on the purpose of this contingent piece of compensation. The chairman viewed it in its original context as an add-on, whereas the human resources executive saw it as an offset to discounted base salaries. The human resources view was closer to the truth, because budgetary pressure on managers throughout the company led to a natural use of this bonus as a bargaining chip in holding down the base salaries of the departmental work forces. When a major acquisition brought a new, and lower, profit structure into this company's portfolio, the "dependable" year-end bonus payments rapidly evaporated, and the workers began earning only their subcompetitive base salaries. So, what the company initially provided to the work force as a risk-free enhancement evolved into a program whose primary purpose was to leverage compensation costs. In this new context of real risk, the stability of the rank-and-file work force was severely threatened.

Medium

The currency of exchange for compensation programs does not vary widely. Stock, cash, and in certain instances, merchandise or travel are the predominant forms of payment. Merchandise and travel incentives, for example, are used almost exclusively in sales organizations for the purposes of directly involving the salesperson's family in the pursuit of a reward and, upon its receipt, allowing the family to experience a personal benefit. In addition, the continuing visible presence of merchandise awards in the recipient's home or office provides a lasting reminder of "a job well done." In setting up these types of programs, it is common practice for companies to put the medium of pay at the hub of the policy wheel and to concentrate on developing the catalog of merchandise and the supporting communication materials while relegating the concerns of setting objectives and measuring performance to secondary status.

Corporations use another noncash form of compensation—stock— for a select group of executives. As noted in the introduction the use of stock in recent years has been rooted as much in the favorable tax treatment of capital gains as in its extended-time-horizon incentive value. In fact, with the enticing tax advantages of the pre-1986 tax reform era, it has been difficult to force an impartial evaluation of the incentive value of a stock-based program. Today, however, the personal and corporate tax advantages have largely been placed on hold, and without these preferences as a distraction, the compensation planner must now be much more circumspect in adopting any stock plan on the premise of its ability to influence management behavior.

Even beyond the tax preference consideration, stock-based compensation may still be favored for reasons that transcend its incentive value. If a corporation is experiencing a cash flow shortage, or if it wants to defer or eliminate the income statement effect of a portion of compensation expense, it will often turn to restricted stock grants or stock options. Though this method of providing added compensation may be well justified by financial circumstances, it should not be taken, prima facie, as an achievement-pay system.

Certainly, under select conditions, almost all of these noncash forms of payment can be used effectively to deliver special "messages" to recipients. More frequently, however, corporations use them to achieve tax preferences or to avoid short-term income statement effects. A policy centered on the medium of pay is, therefore, usually grounded in these nonperformance-related considerations rather than in a true achievement-pay philosophy.

Mechanics

In Alfred Sloan's time, the compensation of an employee was rather simple: a fair day's pay for a fair day's work. But management began to scrutinize the value of the "work," and the link between pay and performance emerged as an equation which was destined to track with commerce itself in its growing complexity. Today, the administrative operating system underlying an incentive program is often viewed as the ultimate criterion for judging its value.

With simplicity of communication and administration as the acid tests for "effectiveness," policymakers often put aside the noble objectives set forth for their achievement-pay system upon discovering that defining and measuring performance is not a straightforward and simple task. They find that paying incentive dollars for more than one objective, or capturing several competing business priorities in an incentive structure, is far too "complex" for their managers' taste. What results is a magnetic attraction to plans that pay for a single financial outcome coupled to a straight-line payout schedule.

This fixation on simple mechanics—second in line to, and maybe even sharing the hub with, organization structure—has been predominant among compensation policymakers in the 1970s and 1980s. Notwithstanding this legacy, the old adage "keep it simple" may now be simpleminded. The volatility of market forces alone may compel the compensation planner to build in a "complex" buffer system to ensure that an incentive plan remains operative under a wide range of market conditions. Furthermore, if there are fundamental trade-offs in performance (e.g., sales growth versus profitability) that a manager must balance on a day-to-day basis, added "complexity" to accommodate these business realities may be necessary. Finally, even without competing business objectives, a manager often has competing time commitments that can be captured using multiple performance measures in an incentive plan. So, any incentive plan that is directly linked to the strategy of a business or to the realities of day-to-day business management will perforce assume a higher level of mechanical complexity in today's commercial environment.

Timing

The timing component of compensation policy is simply the schedule by which payments are released to the employee and, in some instances, the contingent provisions that regulate the release of payments. Timing can be used creatively to secure the loyalty of key personnel during an extended time period, to smooth the earnings of an executive from one year to the next, or to shape the time horizon of a manager's performance planning.

Some companies, for example, will withhold up to one-half of an executive's earned bonus for payment in the succeeding year. So, if bonus earnings fluctuated from $25,000 in the first year to $15,000 in the second year and to $30,000 in year three, actual payouts would be as follows:

Year	Earned Bonus	Bonus Paid			
		Year 1	Year 2	Year 3	Year 4
1	$25,000	$12,500	$12,500	—	—
2	15,000	—	7,500	$ 7,500	—
3	30,000	—	—	15,000	$15,000
Total Paid		$12,500	$20,000	$22,500	$15,000

With this approach, two objectives are accomplished. First, the wide variation in earnings between year two and year three is dramatically reduced; second, the manager has a vested interest in remaining with the company to collect guaranteed bonus earnings in the succeeding year.

Another timing vehicle, most commonly used with stock options or grants, is the vesting schedule. These schedules specify the payment amounts to be made each year and may even specify performance thresholds that the manager must meet to trigger the release of payments. Securing the loyalty of key personnel is usually the primary purpose of these vesting arrangements, but they may also act to influence a manager's planning horizon.

Overlapping long-term incentive cycles is yet another timing mechanism that is used to create continuity and reinforce year-to-year performance consistency. Figure 1.6 illustrates a typical payout pattern for a three-year incentive program. In the first plan cycle, a payout would not be made until year three. However, a second three-year plan cycle would be initiated in year two, and a third cycle in year three, and so forth. These overlapping cycles, therefore, provide a payment each year, once the first plan cycle is completed, and they ensure that, despite business course corrections or changing assumptions, at least one of the long-term incentive cycles remains active.

It is difficult to imagine a management compensation policy with timing at the hub of the wheel—excluding special situations in which retirement programs are partially funded through deferred compensation arrangements. Occasionally, however, sales organizations insist on a schedule of incentive payments that overrides the natural planning and performance cycle (e.g., a monthly payment will be advanced as a credit against a quarterly performance objective), thereby inserting timing in

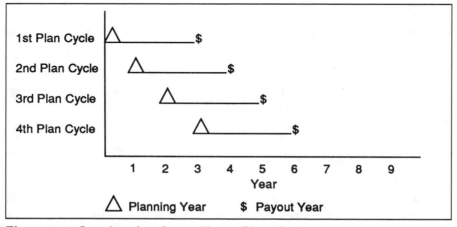

Figure 1.6 Overlapping Long-Term Plan Cycles

the hub. In the final analysis, any compensation policy that is overly concerned with the timing of payments, either for executives or salespeople, is probably sacrificing a more vital focus on performance management.

Performance at the Hub

To make achievement pay work, management must have an unwavering conviction that decisions and priorities are directly influenced by compensation policy. This conviction is demonstrated in action by a CEO's intimate involvement in both the design and the implementation of compensation programs and by the inclusion of compensation planners in the process of formulating business and organization strategies. It is also demonstrated by management's willingness to wrestle with the complexities of performance and to commit to a concrete set of operating plans and strategic bench marks as compensable achievements.

Some might argue that the execution of business strategy, whether at the corporate, business-unit, or functional level, is the essence of performance. Others believe that the cold, hard precipitates of strategy (namely, financial results) are the only valid indicators of how well a business is performing. In this book, neither of these polar views will be accepted; rather, a blend of strategic bench marks and financial results will be consistently advanced as a necessary foundation of achievement pay.

With performance defined in this manner, the fundamental purpose of any achievement-pay system is to influence management's decision-making behavior. In concrete terms, a pay system will govern the locus and ownership of decisions within an organization, and it will regulate the degree of risk and initiative a manager takes in promoting a favored viewpoint. Finally, through the careful design of performance measures, the pay system should affect the manager's mind-set—what factors are considered when a decision is made. (For a detailed discussion of the selection and evaluation of performance criteria and the relationship between performance measures and strategy, see Chapters 4 and 6.)

In contrast to this concept of achievement pay, conventional compensation strategy usually sidesteps the preeminence of management behavior change by using generic financial performance measures that capture only end results, and by presuming that an organization's formal hierarchy accurately reflects how decisions are made at the corporate, business-unit, and functional levels. If, on the other hand, a policy wheel has performance at the hub, it forces critical analyses of the accountabilities not implicit in the organization structure and results in compensation policy groupings, participation criteria, and performance measures that more closely match the management priorities of the company, for each level of business strategy.

The process for developing competitive strategy can be used as the model for building a compensation strategy. A business strategist who matches products to market segments must embrace a view of the product that includes many facets beyond the tangible, physical entity. Packaging, distribution channels, promotional and communications materials, and customer service are just a few of the elements that embody the "product" in its full strategic compass. In this context, the strategist must also intimately know the needs of a targeted market segment and tailor a company's product offering in a way that creates a sustainable competitive advantage.

In like manner, the compensation planner must manipulate the alignment of "product" elements with "market" segments to create an achievement-pay system. The analogs of the product elements are the spokes of the compensation policy wheel, and the market segment analogs are the organizational policy groupings. The planner's analytical process must, therefore, start by uncovering the policy groups that have a common business mission and then proceed to match policy components that cement together the discrete pieces of mission accountability.

Conventional and well-tested compensation and organization concepts are a safe harbor for the compensation planner, even if these concepts are not responsive to business needs and strategies; and internal compensation planners, along with their outside consultants, have tended to ignore the presence of interdepartmental policy groups that fuse a business strategy with its organization and compensation programs. When the bonds among strategy, organization, and compensation remain untested and are tacitly assumed, managers will decide independently what is important to their jobs, how the resources they control will be used, and what interaction they will initiate with other managers in pursuit of their common goals. If, on the other hand, the organization and compensation programs are conceived with performance at the hub, the triad of strategy, organization, and compensation will become a living framework for daily decisions, performance measurement, and individual accountability. In each succeeding chapter of this book, we will examine a separate spoke of the compensation policy wheel to discover how its emphasis in the policy mix should complement varying business missions and strengthen the bonds of the triad.

=== 2 ===

Compensation Newspeak

An anonymous nineteenth-century diplomat once observed, "What appears to be a sloppy or meaningless use of words is often a completely correct use of words to express sloppy or meaningless ideas." This quotation aptly expresses the task at hand: to expand the understanding of compensation policy nuances and to close the gap between precise words and sloppy ideas.

Word Currency

In George Orwell's *1984*, the leaders of Oceania insidiously used words to say one thing in the guise of its opposite. To serve their political aims, the facades of ministry buildings were draped with slogans proclaiming "War Is Peace," "Freedom Is Slavery," "Ignorance Is Strength." Today, politicians have created their version of this ambiguous "Newspeak" by coining phrases like "revenue enhancement" and "user fees" to disguise the less-palatable reality of tax increases. The media world of professional athletics has added yet another facet to this communication art form with a version that has an appealing rhythmic pulse but no discernible meaning.

Their "Nospeak" utterances include: "play good defense and put some points on the board," or "play with intensity and make no mental mistakes."

Not surprisingly, this linguistic legerdemain has invaded the business world, and compensation planners have not been immune. The lexicographers of compensation policy have given us simple words and phrases to describe a compensation program's underpinnings, but if tested against literal usage, a hollow shell of the original meaning is all that remains. Compensation policy vocabulary has changed little in the past 30 years, but its cultivated usage has led to compensation double-talk. In the preceding chapter, some current notions and vocabulary of "pay for performance" have been stripped of their veneer, but before we proceed with the balance of this book a revisionist interpretation of achievement-pay terms is needed.

Lexicon

Competitive pay

> The range of pay levels, discernible in the market, that circumscribe the value of a particular position.

Sam Goldwyn, the noted moviemaker, had a unique interpretation of competitive pay: "We're overpaying him, but he's worth it." In other less iconoclastic circles, however, managers and administrators treat competitive bench marks as immutable absolutes, guarding their "purity" and "truth." Yet a wide variation in market rates of pay can be found for any given position. For example, polling a company's executive search consultants will probably yield the highest rate of pay because members of their labor pool are moving to new employers and expecting a pay increase. Computing an arithmetic mean of published survey data will likely result in a different number than the survey median. (Eliminate the highs and lows from the data base, and another number can be found.) Conducting a custom survey of selected companies, some will argue, yields the most precise definition of competitive pay; and yes, the results of this research will add yet another arrow to the quiver of purity and truth.

So what really is competitive pay? It is the product of a *management consensus* that blends the competing forces of personnel cost control, market pay practices, and an organization's concept of internal pay equity. In light of this natural tension, the compensation planner should not be chagrined by the absence of a pay absolute when discussing competitive pay data. Instead, the planner should work with management to ensure that the competing forces are given proper emphasis at each level in the organization and that the accountability for compensation management is evenly shared between the human resource department and the managers at each organizational level.

Compensation objectives

> Compensation system design criteria that reflect an intimate understanding of an organization's management development needs, business strategy, and leadership style.

Though "attraction, retention, and motivation" bubble forth as the noble objectives of every compensation program, this "Nospeak" term should be forever stricken from the compensation planner's vocabulary—as it has been from every succeeding page of this text. If a company were to articulate its business objectives in an analogous form, it would not be surprising to hear platitudes like "make an acquisition" or "become market-driven." In this broad business context, as well as in the narrower compensation realm, the criteria for judging performance against these types of objectives are ambiguous. Therefore, for compensation objectives to serve a useful purpose in formulating a compensation strategy, they should point candidly to gaps in management or organizational effectiveness, and they should define a clear role for compensation policy in helping to close the gaps. Examples of design criteria that fit this standard include the following:

- Explicitly reinforce a business planning discipline at key levels in the organization.
- Encourage teamwork between design and manufacturing engineering managers.
- Instill an investor perspective in senior managers to encourage a high degree of individual initiative and open debate on critical business policy issues.
- Reinforce a shift in the company's focus from sales growth to account management and development.

Though the compensation strategy implications for any of these statements are not precise, they force a design discipline that constantly reminds the policy planner to question the relevance of any policy element and to trace it to its origin in the objective.

Bonus eligibility criteria ════════════════════════════

A position taxonomy that transcends an organization's formal chain of command and that carefully aligns functional accountability and impact with components of the pay system.

Traditionally, employees have been classified for compensation purposes into administrative and legal groupings (for example, bonus eligible/noneligible; exempt/nonexempt; officer/nonofficer). In addition, salary grades may create a stratification of the employee population. None of these classifications, however, explicitly relates to the context or function of a position. In the absence of this link, organization hierarchy probably dominates compensation policy, and only by chance will any of these classification schemes correlate with the organization's network of mission accountabilities. Recalling the earlier discussion of the compensation policy wheel, this sharp divergence from a pay policy based on organization hierarchy should be a familiar theme. It will be revisited often throughout this book in that it buffets conventional wisdom and progressively constructs a new concept of organizational taxonomy.

Incentive compensation ════════════════════════════

Contingent payments that expressly influence a manager's initiative and, through directional objectives, guide decision-making behavior.

Incentive and *bonus* have been used interchangeably or indiscriminately in the compensation lexicon. As noted previously in our discussion of the Alfred Sloan bonus plan, bonuses are distinguished from incentives by the lack of predefined standards of performance, or by the discretionary nature of the bonus distribution formula. In this book, it is assumed that the simple technology of designing and installing a bonus program is well understood. In fact, accountants and attorneys, unencumbered by any direct reference to a company's organization or strategy, can competently design compensation delivery systems tied to a firm's financial welfare. On the other hand, incentive programs intended to influence management behavior must draw on an integrated view of strategy, organization, and compensation that precisely defines performance at the individual, work team, functional, and corporate levels.

Performance ════════════════════════════

Achievement that truly reflects management's value added—the quality of its judgment in shaping strategy and the proficiency with which the strategy is executed.

Performance is a portfolio of accomplishments, regardless of the size or mission of the unit being measured. The portfolio may include financial ratios, task bench marks, product or market positioning goals, or quality indices. Though it is fashionable to indict management for its failure to advocate this full spectrum of performance dimensions, it is primarily in the realm of incentive compensation that this advocacy breaks down. As a regular routine, any good manager intuitively will check the "trap line" of the full performance portfolio to ensure that the business stays on course. Yet when it comes to variable pay, management's concentration is almost always on end results only.

So, the debate rages whether to mix end results with other performance milestones in incentive pay packages. The strongest argument in favor of a mix is that the impact of some key activities will be felt only long after the end of any particular short-term incentive cycle. Thus, it is necessary to pay for milestone achievements to ensure continuing momentum toward a longer-term objective. Disparaging this argument, however, is the concern that management may incur compensation expense for these milestones in a year of subtarget performance on end results. An equally daunting reconciliation may arise when good performance on end results overshadows meager milestone achievements. Explaining either of these incongruities is a challenge few managers will accept willingly.

In a business environment where management must focus intensely, if not exclusively, on the year-to-year cycle of cash flows and profits, it is difficult to quarrel with a compensation system that pays primarily for the end result. However, for businesses that do not fall into this narrow category, a prime purpose of incentives should be to spotlight the continuity and quality of management's judgment. Through the use of a performance portfolio encompassing the full spectrum of task bench marks and results, changes in tactics and strategy can be brought to center stage, and the trade-offs between long- and short-term performance can be reconciled.

Target performance
> The confidence interval around a planned level of achievement that embodies the imprecision of the planning process.

Many companies establish a single set of numbers as the profile of standard performance for their incentive programs, but it is rare that planning is so precise that these numbers have the unassailable significance with which they are often endowed. It logically follows that incentive systems resting on these pinions of certainty create competition between the managers' desires to maximize their payout opportunity and the integrity of the managers' objective-setting process. If too many dollars ride on the achievement of a performance objective represented by a single number, and if the payouts below this number drop off precipitously, management will be sorely tempted to reduce target performance to its lowest acceptable level and, thereby, increase incentive payouts. The antithesis of this scenario—low incentive earnings thresholds and gradually incremented payout schedules—will lead to a perception of overpayment. Management's reaction, in this case, will likely be to increase performance targets artificially in order to regulate earnings. The unfortunate consequence of either of these scenarios is an erosion in the integrity of the planning process.

Conversely, target performance that is expressed as a confidence interval, matching a company's planning precision, relieves some of the pressure on the objective-setting process. Even more pressure can be relieved if the payout schedules themselves are raised or lowered in accordance with an objective's degree of difficulty. Above all, the definition and usage of target performance should act to strengthen a company's planning process rather than to induce artificial manipulation.

Pay at risk

> The portion of an individual's pay package that is actually contingent on an uncertain result.

Compensation can be structured along a continuous scale from total risk to total guarantee. But any position's compensation must be compared to a standard to determine where on this scale of pay risk the structure lies. This standard comprises two factors: First, *competitive total compensation* is a bench mark that defines the total compensation opportunity at *target* performance. (Thus, to establish a firm concept of pay at risk, target performance must be defined for all positions with a variable compensation component.) Second, the *structure of an incentive program* must be objectively analyzed so that the portion of variable pay that is problematic and the portion that is virtually guaranteed can be determined. With these factors in mind, the amount of pay at risk can be computed as outlined in Figure 2.1.

	Competitive total compensation
Less:	Fixed compensation (base salary)
=	Variable compensation amount
Less:	Warranted portion of variable compensation
=	Pay at risk

Figure 2.1   Pay-at-Risk Calculation

Equity

The impartial application of assessment criteria to determine the value of a position *and* to apportion the guaranteed and at-risk components of compensation.

Compensation science is replete with methods of establishing an equitable ranking of positions within an organization. Some of these approaches allow external market comparisons to dominate the valuation process, whereas others use an internal factor analysis encompassing several "independent" dimensions of a job's intrinsic worth. These approaches can support a base-salary or total-compensation hierarchy that adequately protects position value equity. Left unresolved, though, is the fair determination of pay risk for all positions. Not surprisingly, an organization will commonly rely on its hierarchy as the sole guide for apportioning risk; but this interpretation does not guarantee the proper alignment of pay risk with a position's direct impact on important business missions.

Sales positions have consistently broken this hierarchy barrier, primarily because the variability of their achievements is highly visible, and this variability intuitively corroborates a pay-risk formula superseding the hierarchy. The logic leading to this "special-case" treatment of sales forces is rarely questioned, but it is also rarely applied, in any rigorous manner, to other positions in the organization. If one listens attentively to the rationale underlying this separation of the sales force, it is common to hear such phrases as "direct influence," "proximity to buying decisions," "strategic impact," "customer interface," and so forth. But if a more generic perspective is applied, are there not other positions at similar levels in the organization that can also lay claim to these criteria? The real concern in creating risk equity, therefore, is that the company analyze *all* networks of accountability in an organization to identify positions with comparable impact on a particular mission and to assign consistent levels of pay risk to these positions. Without management's careful attention to this dimension of pay equity, it is unlikely that incentives can play a significant part in strengthening each network's commitment to a mission or its drive for achievement.

On to the Gist

Adam Smith, in his 1981 essay, *Paper Money*, quoted linguist Benjamin Lee Whorf's observations on the Eskimo language when he noted that it contained twenty-seven different words for snow, each connoting another nuance in texture, utility, and consistency; so, the Eskimo's ability to communicate about snow is far greater than ours. The lexicon introduced in this chapter, together with the concepts broached in the introductory comments and "Bedrock" principles, have moved the reader toward a refined vocabulary of compensation policy. Though Newspeak has crept into the everyday world of the compensation planner, a knowing nod of the head to acknowledge a familiar term in this essay can be misleading. "Parrot gabble" has so rounded the corners of today's compensation policy vocabulary that the core lexicon of this book must insist on very precise interpretation. Without this precision, the subtle nuances that form the premise of the book will be lost.

What remains for the succeeding chapters is the application of these terms in a manner that opens the dialogue between management and the technical compensation planners. The prevailing message of all of the preceding discussion is quite simple: Achievement pay is *not* a technical discipline for technocrats; it is, on the contrary, an elemental facet of business policy and competitive strategy firmly implanted in top management's court. From this point on, the discussion centers on practical application and prescription aimed directly at the competitive heart of a business.

3

The Pay Hierarchy Dilemma

Companies customarily use base-salary hierarchies as the foundation of their internal equity and personnel cost-control systems. In a base-salary system, employees at the top of an organization are paid the largest salaries, and base pay decreases at each subordinate level. However, as companies move more aggressively into broad-based achievement-pay programs, this conventional salary hierarchy can be a formidable barrier to proper alignment of compensation mix (base salary versus incentive pay) with position responsibilities. To protect internal equity when at-risk pay is fitted to a particular position and varies throughout an organization, policy planners must breathe new life into a management system that has lain dormant for many years. This system aligns job value with target total compensation rather than with base salary and tailors the pay structure to the distinct needs of various segments of an organization.

Stretching Base Salary

Management's abiding conviction that individual achievement can make a notable difference in company performance has prompted much experimentation with pay systems in an attempt to refine the relationship between personal impact and reward. Within the base-salary arena, however, these advances have been constrained by the rigidity of salary structures tethered to pay rates published in compensation surveys.

In addition to these competitive market ramparts, even the administrative rules for managing base salaries are quite inflexible. Pay progression in a given year is usually bounded by budgets for merit increases and by strict guidelines dependent on an individual's placement in a salary grade range. So, in these times of budgets with modest 4 percent to 5 percent increases, managers have few dollars to spend on outstanding achievement awards, and they may have even fewer dollars for an employee who has, through successive years of good performance, reached the ceiling of a salary range. A manager's flexibility is also limited when individual performance is mediocre: The worst negative action short of termination that a manager can take toward employees in this category is to deny a merit increase; any reduction in base salary is an unspoken taboo.

To counter these pay conventions that only give but do not take away, companies can adopt techniques to formally sanction pay levels above a base-salary grade range. But unlike the familiar procedure of red-circling out of range pay rates, these techniques provide companies with a license to rescind future salary increments if the employee fails to clear the sanctioning hurdles.

Leveraged Merit Increases

In recent years, large companies have snubbed annual cost-of-living adjustments (COLA), and the practice of linking base-salary merit increases to *corporate* performance has gained wider acceptance. Though there are several variations on this theme, a common approach employs a simple formula that adjusts the total merit budget in lockstep with profit levels or with the achievement of specific corporate objectives. A company communicates the parallel structure of merit budget percentages and company performance levels at the beginning of the year, and at the end of the year it sets the actual budget percentage in accordance with the final results. This approach clearly works best with an annual, rather than anniversary, review schedule, but, unlike the technique described next, it can still accommodate the individual performance-evaluation aspect of the merit review process.

In a much publicized program, General Motors attempted to contain the wage spiral of its union work force in the mid-1980s by establishing a sliding scale of wage rates that is adjusted periodically to reflect the operating results of the corporation. Though across-the-board increases are customary in such unionized environments, the possibility of a decrease or freeze in wages based on corporate performance was heralded as an innovative step toward pay for performance.

Another twist to this leveraging concept has been introduced in DuPont's synthetic fiber division. Over a period of three to five years employees gradually increase their contributions to an at-risk pool. This pool is funded by their normal salary increases, and at the final stage of implementation it will represent about 6 percent of pay. Year-end bonuses are based on how the division performs relative to its annual earnings target. If the division meets its objectives, a full rebate of the 6 percent contribution is granted; if the objective is surpassed, employees can earn up to an additional 12 percent. If performance falls below 80 percent of the objective, however, the pool is lost. The jury is still out, however, on whether this type of profit-sharing program truly affects employee behavior or whether it is merely a cost-control initiative masquerading as an "incentive."

Lump-Sum Merit Award

Another advance in base-salary management is the funding of a reserve account for special year-end bonus awards that are designated for a small group of meritorious employees. Unlike the leveraged merit pool technique, this pool is budgeted as a part of payroll expense and is not contingent on total company performance.

A large telecommunications utility has used this type of program for many years. Instead of adding individual bonus plans at each successive level in the organization, the utility supplements its traditionally small merit increase budgets with this discretionary form of compensation. Each year, managers convene to evaluate individual performance and agree on how the merit awards should be distributed. On the surface, this appears to be a fair and motivational program. But a more penetrating look reveals that the motivational impact of the program is diluted by political intrigue and the absence of any predefined performance criteria. With a fixed lump-sum merit budget and stringent quotas on the percentage of employees that can participate in the program, the evaluation sessions have degenerated into a quagmire of infighting and negotiation between the managers for reciprocal treatment of favored employees. Over time, a well-worn pattern of repeat recipients, together with the discretionary, after-the-fact performance criteria, has fueled much cynical commentary on the program.

This utility company provides an example of a reasonably sound pay concept gone awry due to bureaucracy and management's desertion of its original performance-management precepts. In the right operating environment, where the organization structure is relatively flat and individual performance-management systems are entrenched, managers can use lump-sum merit awards to hold fixed salary costs down while rewarding a few select employees for their outstanding contributions. Similar only in theme to its broader-based cousin, the performance bonus, the lump-sum merit award program focuses exclusively on extraordinary performers, and if communicated properly it can create role models of excellence throughout the organization.

Another variation on the lump-sum merit concept has been employed by two major health care facilities. In their version, salary ranges are capped at the midpoint of a conventional salary range. The upper end of the range is paid out in quarterly bonuses in the following year and is based on each individual's performance evaluation. So an employee who performed at a better than competent level receives the target base salary plus a performance bonus. However, unlike typical salary increases, which take the form of "a gift that keeps on giving," employees are required to *earn* above competitive compensation each successive year; but the number of employees participating in the program is not arbitrarily restricted as in the utility company example.

Red-Circled Job Evaluations

Normally, if an individual is paid more than the maximum of his or her assigned pay grade, an alarm system is triggered that calls into action a special administrative procedure. Commonly known as *red-circling*, this procedure places severe constraints on merit increases for the individual or, on the opposite end of the spectrum, may formally grant a dispensation from the standard merit-increase policy and allow the individual to receive raises that continue to widen the overpayment gap.

The history behind any red-circled rate of pay is usually attributable to one of four conditions:

■ **Structural Revision.** If a salary-administration structure has not been maintained properly through at least biennial updates, or if it has fallen into a state of disuse, a reinstitution of the system will frequently highlight positions or individuals whose compensation has lost touch with the marketplace. When red-circled rates are purely the result of administrative abuse, a period of a pay freeze will usually bring the rates in line with the revised structure. Occasionally, however, actual pay reductions, over a two- or three-year phased schedule, may be necessary. With this latter approach, an annual upgrading of the company's pay structure is combined with small reductions in the employee's pay to accelerate the closing of the overpayment gap. (As a practical matter, however, pay rates are rarely reduced, even when new structures are implemented.)

▌ **Demotion.** The "D-word," though unpalatable to all affected parties, is a fact of life in organizations that change quickly and frequently. Moreover, with the increasing emphasis on employment security for both the exempt and hourly work forces, demotions are likely to become more prevalent. A particularly sensitive question involves what to pay an individual who has been demoted. Depending on the gap between the individual's current pay level and the newly assigned pay grade maximum, wage freezes or phased reductions may be in order.

▌ **Labor Market Scarcity.** The demand for technical labor often reaches periodic highs. In recent years, for example, the markets for data-processing and biotechnology-engineering personnel have been overheated. Similarly, in the late 1970s and in the late 1980s the management-consulting and investment-banking industries went to war over MBA graduates from elite East Coast business schools, creating an imbalance in supply and demand; as in any free market, prices were caught in a severe updraft.

These labor-pool shortages can play havoc with a company's internal compensation administration system if special policies are not put in place to guide the recruiting and merit-review activities. When a company's internal structure does not keep pace with these specialized labor markets, the pay levels of newly hired employees will creep up and eventually threaten the integrity of the entire structure. Moreover, failing to raise the pay levels of incumbents at a rate comparable to that in the competitive market may leave a company vulnerable to the predatory recruiting of its scarcest personnel resources.

To break this cycle, a formal *market value divergence policy* can be established that essentially red-circles the grading of a job rather than its pay rates. With this approach, the company establishes criteria to classify jobs into one of four categories for the purpose of labor-market comparison (Figure 3.1). The determinants of a position's labor market relate to its career path and to the primary influence on pay progression along the career path. For example, generic labor market data should be used when a position's career path can cross industry boundaries, and job scope is a dominant pay influence. Filtering all of the positions in an organization through this screen will likely yield two or three groups of positions that clearly fall into the specialized market categories (that is, industry-family, industry-specific, or job-family specific.)

The final step in creating a market-value divergence policy is to quantify the differences between labor markets. Using industry- or discipline-specific surveys, companies can compare competitive pay rates for bench-mark jobs with the generic labor-market standard. If differences of more than 8 percent to 12 percent are discovered in this comparison, it is likely that a permanent upgrade of the position (Figure 3.2) is necessary to ensure an externally competitive rate of pay.

| | Position Determinants of Market Value | |
Labor Markets	Career Path Constraints	Pay Progression Correlates
General	Career path can cross unrelated industries	Job scope is primary correlate of pay level
Industry-Family	Career path constrained to related industries (e.g., pharmaceutical, chemical)	Functional experience is primary correlate of pay level
Industry-Specific	Depth of industry knowledge is primary correlate of pay level	Career path is exclusive to the industry
Job Family–Specific	Career path is exclusive to the discipline (i.e., rarely ascends to general management)	Depth of technical discipline knowledge is primary correlate of pay level

Figure 3.1   Classification of Labor Markets

Example: Pharmaceutical Industry Plant General Manager

Internal Pay Grade	Salary Range		Competitive Medians	
	Minimum	Maximum	Generic[a]	Specialized[b]
5	$46,000	$69,000		$56,800
4	40,000	60,000	$51,500	

[a]General industry.
[b]Pharmaceutical.

Figure 3.2   Special Labor-Market Upgrade

▌**Strategic Importance.** Even after a compensation planner has pinpointed the relevant labor market for a particular position, the external factors that suggest its pay grade may still not reflect the circumstances that are unique to the company's business strategy. Though job evaluation criteria effectively capture the know-how, accountability, and problem-solving dimensions of a position, they are relatively insensitive to the demands that some strategies place on opportunistic acquisition of special talents. For example, a pharmaceutical or electronics company may pay little attention to either external or internal pay restrictions if a notable expert suddenly becomes available. In like manner, a financial services company will usually pull out all the stops to acquire a well-connected "rainmaker." And a company on the brink of extinction will usually disregard its formal pay structure in trying to woo a key manager for a critical function.

The rationale behind these pay decisions is rarely formalized; and in the absence of a policy, there is a good chance that each manager faced with a new challenge will argue for the special treatment of a favored employee or an open-ended budget for a new hire. To consistently test the foundation of these arguments and to prove the strategic importance of a position, screening criteria such as those listed in Figure 3.3 should be used.

In the example analysis shown in Figure 3.4, the vice presidents of commercial development and research and development would be slotted in a salary grade according to the third quartile of competitive data. As in the example for special labor-market upgrades (Figure 3.2), this third quartile red-circled slotting would likely result in the assignment of a salary grade at least one notch up from the grade prescribed by the competitive median.

— 51 —

Criteria	Applicability			
	High (3)	Moderate (2)	Low (1)	None (0)
Little or no opportunity for training—performance in job must be at high level immediately				
The results of job performance can be critically linked to the strategic success of the company				
The life cycle of the job is limited to 2 to 3 years				
The replacement costs (not just financial) of the position are high due to company experience or specific project knowledge that is required				
A new position is created due to market availability of a unique talent				
Company's industry position or reputation affects size of available labor pool				

Figure 3.3 Tests for Strategic Importance

In the Harold Geneen era of large diversified holding companies, the concept of formal strategic and market value divergence pay policies would have been particularly useful. With a portfolio of companies spanning such disparate enterprises as restaurants and oil drilling, these conglomerates could have employed the divergence concepts to accommodate the eclectic pay requirements of their subsidiaries. For the sake of administrative simplicity, however, a policy of compensation homogeneity was most frequently imposed. Unfortunately, the residue from these misguided policies continues to plague many of today's subsidiaries whose specialized industry pay practices legitimately differ from those of general industry.

Importance Evaluation Criteria

Position	Limited Opportunity	Direct Linkage to Strategic Results	Time-Limited Job Life Cycle	High Replacement Costs	Unique Talent Availability	Labor Pool Dependent on Industry Stature	Total Evaluation Points
Production supervisor	1	0	0	1	0	0	2
Vice president—commercial development	3	3	1	3	1	3	14
Manager—acquisitions	3	2	2	1	2	1	11
Manager—information technology	3	1	3	1	2	0	10
Vice president—research and development	3	3	1	3	2	3	15
Scientist	2	0	0	1	0	1	4

Total Evaluation Points	Market Pricing Guidelines
0–5	First quartile
6–12	Median
13–18	Third quartile

Figure 3.4 Example of Strategic Importance Analysis

Consider, for example, a large British holding company with dominant interests in bulk chemicals and industrial supplies that attempted to force-fit all of its companies into a single base-salary structure. The small pharmaceutical subsidiary of this company fought a continuing war of attrition with the parent over the subsidiary's offbeat compensation structure until the parent exercised its "pocket" veto. At that point, the subsidiary's vice president of human resources recognized that the debate on these compensation issues needed to move from the realm of mere opinion and assumption to that of strategic imperatives. The system of market divergence and strategic importance screening outlined previously was used to provide a common language for the human resource departments of the parent and subsidiary companies. With this common ground established, they could assess the competitive pressures in the market and objectively evaluate each position for special treatment.

A Cafeteria of Pay Structures

As an administrative convenience, many companies choose to create two salary structures—one for exempt personnel and a separate one for the hourly work force. To place positions in these structures, the company applies uniformly throughout the organization some type of salary system whose purpose is to equitably rank the value of jobs. Most of these evaluation systems, such as factor comparison, point-factor, whole-job ranking, and regression analysis, have a built-in bias toward a managerial career track. Though this bias is not inherent in the mechanics of the techniques (with the possible exception of regression analysis, for which the independent variables are organization factors such as reporting level and number of subordinate levels), the implicit or explicit weighting of evaluation criteria inevitably reflects the vested interests of the managers designing or applying the systems. Following this vein, one could project that if scientists, engineers, or salespeople designed these job-evaluation models, the biases would probably have a different flavor.

This is not to imply that any organizational faction charged with the responsibility for design is incapable of objectivity. On the contrary, the bias is unquestionably appropriate for some segments of an organization. The policy planner must therefore choose either a single scaling system that creates a mediocre fit with the career progression in *all* organizational segments, or a family of scaling systems that fits the individual characteristics of each organizational segment. Quite simply, if the evaluation or reward system encourages a person to seek managerial responsibilities when doing so is not in the best interests of either the company or the employee, then clearly a different basis for the hierarchy of rewards is necessary for these strategically important nonmanagerial positions.

Some notable examples of functions that require this special treatment are probably familiar to most readers:

■ **Engineering/Research and Development.** Conventional pay hierarchies in technical organizations often block advancement opportunities for highly skilled personnel who are either uninterested in or incapable of assuming managerial positions. A parallel job-evaluation system and salary structure that equates technical skill with managerial skill allows for the continuing progression of these valued employees, and it insulates them from the pressure to accept supervisory positions in order to move into higher pay grades.

A typical dual career ladder is illustrated in Figure 3.5. In this parallel progression, note that senior technical personnel move through steps in the salary structure in the same manner as those on a managerial track. The primary difference, however, is that the criteria that govern promotions on the technical side of the ladder (and that implicitly rank the value of the positions) are related to technical competence, professional visibility, and project-management accomplishments rather than supervisory and administrative skills.

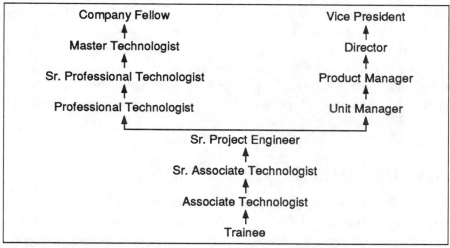

Figure 3.5 Technology Organization: Dual Career-Ladder Example

▌ **Sales Force.** Sales representatives and managers are often ill-fitting cogs in the machinery of classic base-salary hierarchies. Unlike most middle- and lower-level positions in an organization, incentive programs make up a significant portion of the total pay package for these positions. Moreover, conventional job evaluation criteria rarely capture the importance or differentiate among the various types of external relationship-management and interpersonal skills that determine the value of a selling job. Therefore, many companies have created separate salary structures and progression criteria with which to manage the pay of their sales personnel. Usually, these criteria fall into three categories, planning, selling, and administration, each of which is divided into distinct levels of competence and progression in skills.

▌ **Shop Floor Personnel.** Peter Drucker, among many others, has touted the advantages of skill-based pay systems for hourly personnel. A skill-based approach is particularly supportive of manufacturing work-cell organizations that depend on aggressive cross-training programs for their effectiveness. In a work-cell system, job value and pay grades are driven by the portfolio of skills the employee masters rather than by the characteristics of a particular task assigned to the individual.

Despite the obvious benefits of these specialized pay hierarchies, compensation planners still more commonly homogenize rather than diversify their portfolios of job-ranking systems. However, administering compensation with a limited arsenal can dull a company's competitive edge and preempt any meaningful form of achievement pay. Therefore, as companies look toward the future for a way to aggressively support their strategic initiatives with organization-building compensation policies, the enlightened proliferation of specialized job-scaling systems will be an important plank in the strategic policy platform of a company's human resources department.

Moving to a Higher Plane

Though noteworthy, the advances in base-salary management that have just been examined still fall short of the comprehensive reform that is required for business to embrace the full compass of achievement pay. Like so many good ideas in the compensation discipline that enjoy widespread theoretical discourse but are dismissed too readily because of their complexity or the threat of disruptive change that they pose, the idea of a *total-compensation hierarchy* has suffered a quiet demise. Contributing to this fate was the attempt by compensation planners to apply the concept to all positions in an organization. Forgetting that even the tried-and-true base-salary hierarchy is a misfit for certain segments of the organization (for example, sales and marketing), these planners quickly reversed course when confronted with a function or group of positions that did not fit the total-compensation mold.

So, as the first step in adopting an achievement-pay philosophy, total compensation must be disinterred as a practical, and even necessary, basis for managing internal equity for certain segments of a company. With this concept, a compensation hierarchy is built around each position's total compensation at target, or standard, performance. Thus, positions in the same compensation grade may, depending on their nature, have substantially different compensation mix (and, in turn, widely varying base salaries).

Referring to Figure 3.6, it can be noted that at target performance, a position is paid competitive total compensation. (The actual target rate of pay is based on the normal blend of external market and internal equity

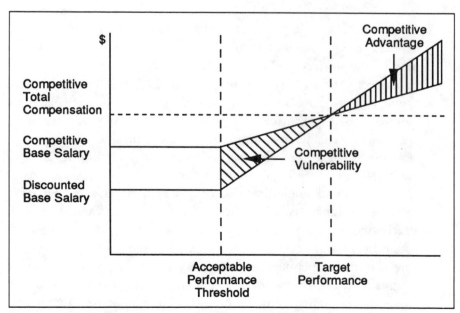

Figure 3.6 Alternative Compensation Hierarchies

considerations.) Base salary, though, is determined by the slope of a position's incentive payout schedule rather than competitive base-salary data or job-evaluation results. For example, if a company's philosophy is to provide above-market pay for outstanding performance, it is likely that its base salaries are discounted from competitive salary rates to partially counterbalance an accelerated incentive schedule. Therefore, at substandard performance, an individual in a total-compensation hierarchy may be paid less than others with a competitive base salary, potentially exposing the company to predatory recruitment. Conversely, when performance is above target, the individual is paid more than peers on a competitive salary plan, thereby providing the company with a protective cushion against predatory recruiters. This risk-reward chemistry is at the heart of achievement-pay, and it is inescapable that both the company and the individual confront these trade-offs when this compensation philosophy is adopted.

The Rewards of Total Compensation

A company that is dominated by sales and marketing activities and that speaks with conviction about the impact individual positions have on the execution of the company's strategy is well suited to a total-compensation hierarchy. Some specific examples come to mind:

▌ Company A, a large personal-computer distribution and retailing concern, recognizes that company sales are not the exclusive province of the dealer-development function and that other positions also directly influencing sales results—purchasing and product management—must have a stake in the success of the dealer network.

▌ Company B, a pharmaceutical firm, is, like most pharmaceutical companies, actually two separate entities: a product-development laboratory and a sales and marketing house. Even the legal- and medical-affairs support personnel fit securely under product management's broad umbrella. The only way a pharmaceutical firm recovers its sunk cost in research and development and generates a satisfactory return for its stockholders is by nurturing a sense of commitment and urgency across this wide range of functions involved in the launching and management of new products.

▌ Company C, a software-development house, like the pharmaceutical model, has a highly technical development arm and an integrated sales and marketing function made up of pure selling as well as specialized customer-support personnel. The successful sale of the company's extremely complex and expensive software system relies on closely orchestrated presale and postsale customer support. A special admixture of cohesion and independent accountability within the account-management team is essential to the company's welfare.

In each of these situations, the sales mission is shared by many other functions that contribute measurably to the accomplishment of revenue and profitability goals. And other positions outside this network of mission accountability—human resources, accounting, and control—still serve all segments of the organization in a purely support capacity. Each of these companies quickly discovered that a compensation-risk policy coupled exclusively with a base-salary hierarchy would ignore the important distinctions in accountability and individual contribution inherent in the operating environments of their teams and that such a policy would give rise to inequitable distribution of compensation risk.

Recalling an earlier discussion of job evaluation in this chapter, internal equity at these companies was protected by an alignment of the pay structures with competitive practices and an objective ranking of position requirements within the organization. But since base salary rather than total compensation at target performance was matched to this ranking, any attempt to vary compensation risk within a given tier of the structure would distort total compensation equity by scrambling the actual pay opportunities at target performance.

Suppose the ranking had been matched to target total compensation, then a new dimension of compensation equity could be defined, and at-risk pay could be more flexibly used to reflect a position's direct impact on performance. With these distinct advantages of this new hierarchy, the policy planner reaps added benefits to support an achievement-pay philosophy:

▮ With more compensation at risk for critical positions, a company can use a wider variety of incentive-performance measures to better reinforce strategic priorities. An axiom of incentive compensation states that "the booty must fit the feat." Too small a reward for too large an effort usually has little influence on behavior. Thus, if an individual manager must balance several key objectives, it is crucial that a sufficient amount of incentive pay be available to spread among the competing priorities.

▌ A culture that nurtures risk taking and attracts aggressive managers can be an important by-product of a more highly leveraged compensation system. Nonetheless, some members of elite board-compensation committees have argued that the volatility induced by highly leveraged compensation progrms will become less acceptable in the future. They believe that post-1992 Europe will pose a dual threat to U.S. industry's competitive strength: world labor markets will become more homogeneous; and the bidding for experienced management talent will intensify.

In the words of the modern-day author and economist Adam Smith, "There is probably a group of cells somewhere in the cerebral cortex that resonates to the fear of the unknown; of the enemy tribe over the horizon; of strange men on horseback burning barns." Yet the legacy of U.S. industry has been to react aggressively to these unseen demons with imagination and ingenuity. But there is nothing imaginative about risk-free pay packages and their nurturing of the 1980's era of complacency. This book's precepts therefore are unequivocal in their support of greater, rather than less, real risk in executive pay.

Ministerial Alterations

Compared to today's base-salary management procedures, total-compensation administration adds a degree of complexity to the compensation planner's domain. The first departure from the past involves the building of systems to manage ranges of *expected* compensation rather than fixed dollar amounts constrained by salary-grade boundaries and survey medians. Also, human resources planning takes on added intricacy when an organization is stratified into position categories that violate the gaited progression of base salaries and pay risk. These administrative accommodations are summarized under the following broad headings.

Describing Pay Risk

Because of computational convenience, incentive-compensation nomenclature defines the portion of pay placed at risk as a percentage of base salary. But from a philosophical viewpoint, this emphasis is misplaced. A manager with a base salary of $50,000 and target total compensation of $75,000 has been conditioned to think of the award for achieving target performance as 50 percent of base salary. Actually, this award is only 33 percent if expressed as a percentage of total compensation. This alternative expression keynotes the company's focus on target total compensation in its pay-management philosophy.

Although this restatement may seem a minor distinction, this subtle change in nomenclature has proven to be far more disconcerting to companies undergoing the conversion than many of the other more substantive aspects of the total-compensation system. In light of this experience, the balance of this chapter uses the familiar base-salary denominator—more to avoid the potential distraction of new arithmetic than to discount the communication value of this change in perspective.

Pricing the Structure

Companies rely on published compensation surveys as their competitive data base, and these surveys usually provide both base-salary and total-compensation information. Confronted with this choice, most compensation planners opt for a base-salary comparison, because this index is less sensitive to both individual and industry performance. When a company chooses a total-compensation approach, however, it must expand the competitive data base and track two or three successive years of total-compensation data as the foundation for the internal structure. If a time series is used, the effects of industry performance cycles on the data base will be reduced and the compensation planner will gain a more precise awareness of actual *target* total compensation, as illustrated in Figure 3.7.

External Recruitment

As discussed earlier, a total-compensation system usually results in certain positions having base salaries somewhat below market levels. When re-

Position: Division Vice President
Survey Medians ($000)

Survey Year	Base Salary	Total Compensation	Percentage Spread
1989	$122	$153	25%
1988	115	135	17
1987	106	129	22

1990 base salary projection (+6%) = $129
Average spread (22%) = 28

1990 projected target total compensation = $157

Spread = difference between base salary and total compensation

Figure 3.7   Time Series Analysis of Competitive Data

cruiting in the open market for these positions, the compensation planner at some point will undoubtedly come under severe pressure to abandon the chosen compensation policy in favor of a "competitive" base salary. Succumbing to this pressure, however, is fatal to the total-compensation basis of internal equity and to the achievement-pay philosophy it supports. Therefore, the compensation planner's first allegiance in these circumstances must be to the company's compensation mix policy and its inherent selection bias for risk-taking personnel.

Recognizing that it would be foolish to rigidly enforce this type of policy and allow no compromise, a company should offer a graduated base-salary program to ease the recruited manager's transition. A market-competitive base salary is provided during the phase-in period and is gradually stepped down as the individual becomes fully integrated into the organization. Since the at-risk portion of pay is not reduced during the transition period, the subsidy portion of base salary should be treated as an offset to any incentive earnings. In this way compensation equity is protected throughout the transitional period.

Merit Reviews

When a large portion of compensation is at risk, it is only natural for base-salary management and its associated merit-review cycle to slip out of view. But incentives can be expected to focus on only a small fraction of a position's accountabilities, and it would be foolish to argue that the measurement of a manager's achievements starts and stops within the boundaries of the incentive plan. Nor would it be prudent to reduce the merit-increase process to the mere administration of a cost-of-living adjustment. So, to bring the full spectrum of a position's accountabilities back into view, it is crucial that the company preserve the potency of the salary-review process.

To achieve this end, either of two approaches can be used. If bonuses are variable dollar amounts (rather than percentages of base salary that automatically apportion an increase to each component of pay), or if they are stated as a percentage of a salary-grade midpoint, merit increases can be split proportionately between base salary and target incentive to increase the leverage of the merit increase. Or the importance of the salary increase can be amplified further if the salary advances are deferred for two or three years so that the merit pool builds to a sufficient level to counterbalance the incentive bias of the compensation structure. To ensure that individual performance management does not become flaccid during this extended merit-review cycle, periodic performance-counseling sessions should continue. Instead of rewarding base-salary increments at these interim sessions, however, a company can establish a bank for accumulating performance credits to track the individual's performance record and to serve as the basis for the biennial or triennial merit increase.

Career Path Management

When compensation mix is tailored to each position, base-salary inversions or exaggerated salary progressions can occur along natural career paths, particularly when a high-incentive-mix job feeds into a lower-incentive-mix job, or vice versa. A practical solution to this dilemma, illustrated in Figure 3.8, starts with the identification of critical career progressions. Once these are identified and the total compensation and mix data are plotted in the progression map, discontinuities should become obvious. In the example, the skills acquired in the national accounts– or regional sales–management jobs qualify an individual for the position of either director of operations or dealer development manager. Based on the provisional total-compensation and mix assignments for these positions, the high-risk package of the dealer development position poses recruiting barriers.

Thus, in the process of implementing a new total-compensation system, the planner must decide whether to make permanent base-salary adjustments to both the feeder and the target positions to close the base-salary gap, or whether to use a graduated-salary program similar to the one recommended for external recruitment transitions. The planner's course of action for the sample scenario would probably include both techniques—modest risk adjustments for the area national account manager and the dealer development manager to narrow the gap, and the transitional program for any incumbents who take this career step. The other progressions in this career map do not create significant problems and should be left as they were originally designed.

Benefits Integration

Frequently, employee benefits programs are based on formulas that consider base salaries alone and do not include incentive payments when the size of a particular benefit, such as long-term disability, life-insurance coverage, or retirement pensions, is calculated. When an achievement-pay program substantially increases the amount of incentive pay for selected positions, a company can avoid the attendant reduction in benefits

Provisional Policy

Feeder Positions				Target Positions			
	Total Compensation	Base Salary	Risk Percentage of Base Salary		Total Compensation	Base Salary	Risk Percentage of Base Salary
Area national account manager	$53,000	$43,000	23%	Director of operations	$68,000	$44,000	55%
Regional manager	$57,000	$38,000	50%	Dealer development manager	$68,000	$35,000	94%

Permanent Policy

Area national account manager	$53,000	$39,000	36%	Director of operations	$68,000	$44,000	55%
Regional manager	$57,000	$38,000	50%	Dealer development manager	$68,000	$39,000	74%

Figure 3.8 Sample Career Progression Map

with simple alterations to the formula. One way would be to simply substitute target total compensation in the formula for base salary. As a practical matter, however, costs of benefits would increase proportionately to the target incentive payment and would inevitably provide some employees with a benefit that was not earned.

A more even-handed approach would be to base the benefit on actual total compensation. Though the benefit costs would still increase to about the same level as for the target total-compensation approach, this alternative would more equitably link benefits to performance. Tying benefits to performance in this manner has not received much air time and might initially be perceived by employees as a reduction in benefit levels.

Another, and perhaps the most balanced, alternative is to assign a fixed basis for the benefit formula (for example, the midpoint of the total-compensation range) to each grade in the structure. This approach not only ensures a fairer determination of benefits than a salary-based formula, but it also gives the company a firm grip on the costs of its nonwelfare benefits programs while guaranteeing stable benefit levels to the employees.

Living through Implementation: A Case Example

A large commercial finance corporation, following the initiatives of its new management team, embarked on a program of broad-based diversification of its services. To implement its strategy, the company made major organizational changes that resulted in a highly visible stratification of functional accountabilities. Not surprisingly, the marketing (or, in the commercial finance jargon, *origination*) function was at the pinnacle of the organization. Next in order was the operations or account management function, where the loans were monitored on a day-to-day basis. The credit and administrative support functions fell in beneath operations.

It was the conviction of top management that the leverage (at-risk pay) in the company's compensation system should reflect this ranking of functional impact throughout all levels of the organization. In specific terms, marketing personnel should consistently have a greater total-compensation opportunity than personnel in other functions, but at target performance, originators should be paid about the same as account managers. Credit personnel should have most of their compensation guaranteed, since the integrity of their judgments is crucial to the quality of the loan portfolio, but their target total compensation should be only slightly less than that of their peers in the operations function. Finally, it was decided that staff personnel should have most of their compensation guaranteed, except at the senior corporate levels where added risk is affordable and the policy impact of the positions justifies a significant incentive component.

A second dimension of this stratification relates to the differences among the corporation's commercial finance market segments. At one end of the spectrum, the firm's large corporate finance and transportation equipment deals were more complex and highly profitable and were usually discrete, one-time opportunities. In contrast, its consumer business was characterized by much-smaller loans and lower profitability but a more renewable and steady source of income. Consequently, it was decided that risk should also vary within a function across these business lines.

Translating these mandates into a concrete compensation mix policy yielded the provisional guidelines illustrated in Figure 3.9. Given the diversity of this risk policy and the relative compression of target total-compensation levels, a conventional base-salary hierarchy was clearly impractical. So the next step was to build a total-compensation structure and to assign positions to grades (see Figure 3.10). Unlike a base-salary structure, this total-compensation grading system includes three distinct sectors for each grade range. The first sector is from the "threshold" to the minimum of the meeting-expectations range; it makes up 25 percent of the total range. Entry-level employees or those performing at substandard levels would normally fall into this sector. Most of the employees,

Incentive Class	At-Risk Pay (Target Percentage of Base Salary)	
	Consumer	Commercial
Origination	33%	100%
Account management	20	25
Credit and administration	5	10
	Staff	Line
Senior management	25%	45%
General corporate	5–10	NA

Figure 3.9 Provisional Risk Policy

Compensation Grade	Threshold	Meeting-Expectations Range		Target Limit
		Minimum	Maximum	
10	$149,600	$174,600	$224,400	$249,300
9	132,900	149,600	182,800	199,400
8	110,800	124,800	152,400	166,200
7	95,200	105,400	125,500	135,600
6	81,000	89,700	106,800	115,400
5	71,000	77,400	89,800	96,100
4	61,800	67,400	78,200	83,600
3	53,700	58,600	68,000	72,700
2	48,100	51,600	58,400	61,800
1	42,700	45,900	51,900	55,000

Figure 3.10   Extract from Total Compensation Structure

however, would be paid in the meeting-expectations range of their grade, which accounts for 50 percent of the total range. The top end of any grade is bounded by a "target limit" rather than a maximum (as in conventional base-salary structures), since each department's incentive plan was designed with an uncapped earnings potential. The target limit thereby serves as a ceiling on the amount that can be paid to any position in the grade for achieving target performance, and this sector of the compensation range is reserved for the small number of employees that qualify as outstanding performers.

Using a combination of survey data on total-compensation levels and an internal whole-job ranking of positions, the corporation placed each job in a total-compensation grade. Base salaries were then set considering the position's incentive-class assignment and each individual's performance record. For example, an account executive was assigned to grade 4 with a target incentive of 20 percent of base salary and was placed near the top of the meeting-expectations range based on her performance record. Thus, with a total compensation target of $77,500, her base salary was set at $64,600 ($77,500 divided by 1.2).

To manage base salaries into the future, a special policy was defined that allocates merit increases based on the assigned total-compensation sector and the individual's actual incentive earnings (see Figure 3.11). So if the account executive starting the year with target compensation in the meeting-expectations range was to earn 130 percent of her target incentive, she would qualify for up to 150 percent of the budgeted merit

Merit-Increase Percentage of Merit Budget

Assigned Target Total Compensation Sector	Actual Incentive-Earnings Percentage of Target Incentive		
	0%–60	61%–125%	126+%
Minimum acceptable	Up to 50% of budget	Up to 125% of budget	Up to 200% of budget
Meeting expectations	No increase	Up to budgeted increase	Up to 150% of budget
Outstanding	No increase	No increase	Up to 125% of budget

Figure 3.11 Base-Salary Merit-Increase Guidelines

Grade	Meeting Expectations Minimum	Position Assigned	Target Risk	Minimum Base Salary
6	$89,700	Vice president–marketing and sales	45%	$61,900
		Vice president–client services	25	71,800
		Vice president–operations (commercial)	20	74,800
5	77,400	Regional sales manager	55	49,900
		Vice president–marketing	45	53,400
		Product manager	33	58,200
		Account executive	20	64,500
		Corporate credit manager	10	70,400
4	67,400	Area manager	45	46,500
		Regional operations manager	20	56,200
		Vice president–operations (consumer)	20	56,200
		Senior underwriter	10	61,300
		Audit manager	10	61,300

Figure 3.12 Extract from Position Grade Assignment

Code	Condition	Policy
1	Incentive opportunity increased—target total compensation is more than 15% above Meeting Expectations Maximum	Reduce base salary immediately, or freeze base salary for an extended period with a graduated incentive increase
2	Incentive opportunity increased—target total compensation is more than Meeting Expectations Maximum, but by less than 15%	Base salary frozen until target total compensation matches performance sector
3	Incentive opportunity increased—target total compensation is between Threshold and Meeting Expectations Maximum	Some base salary increase is possible if performance warrants an upgrade of the individual's compensation sector
4	Incentive opportunity increased—target total compensation is below Threshold	Accelerated base-salary review schedule is required to bring target compensation within grade boundaries
5	Incentive opportunity reduced—target total compensation is more than 15% above Meeting Expectations Maximum	Consider immediate reduction in base salary
6	Incentive opportunity reduced—target total compensation is more than Meeting Expectations Maximum, but by less than 15%	Base salary frozen until target total compensation matches performance sector
7	Incentive opportunity reduced—target total compensation is between Threshold and Meeting Expectations Maximum	Some base salary increase is possible to fully or partially offset the incentive opportunity reduction
8	Incentive opportunity reduced—target total compensation is below Threshold	Accelerated base salary review schedule is required to bring target compensation within tier boundaries

Figure 3.13   Implementation Policy Guidelines

increase. In contrast, if another account executive, also placed in the middle sector of the range was to earn only 30 percent of the target incentive, no base salary increase would be given. This policy was necessary to ensure that employees did not ride a succession of base-salary increases into a performance sector that was unwarranted by their performance records. It was strengthened by a further provision that employees remaining in the bottom sector of a range for more than two years were automatically assigned probationary status.

To demonstrate the dramatic impact of the total-compensation policy as well as the implementation challenge it presents, Figure 3.12 lists the grade assignments of several positions in the new structure and the associated base-salary levels. It is apparent from this exhibit that even though at-risk pay was matched rigorously to the varying types of jobs within a grade, internal equity was not sacrificed. However, to bring about the transition from the existing base-salary administration system, the corporation had to correct many anomalies in base pay. Figure 3.13 summarizes eight separate categories into which all employees fell and prescribes an implementation policy tailored to each scenario. Note that because this company's base-salary structure was unattended for an extended period and because the new program introduced major changes in the at-risk portion of pay, both up and down, a small group of positions suffered base-salary reductions, which were phased in over a two- or three-year period.

==== 4 ====

Performance Units

Where the Buck Stops

A position's base salary, or its organizational reporting level, most frequently is the basis for the position's placement in one of the company's various incentive participation (or non-participation) groups. This book's persistent criticism of such mechanistic formulation of policy should by now sound familiar. Carrying this critical perspective further, incentive eligibility based on organization hierarchy may create an appealing architectural parlance, but it usually ignores the vertical and cross-functional alliances intrinsic in a company's mission.

An exception to this general observation is the treatment of sales forces as distinct compensation policy units. Because the mission and results of sales activity seem obvious and measurable, it has been natural for companies to segregate their selling units and give them special compensation arrangements. Other organizational clusters, such as product- or account-management teams, have also been recognized as special-accountability units, but they are not typically given the distinct compensation consideration accorded the sales function. Arm in arm, compensation planners and senior management have turned their backs on the obvious contradictions embodied in these examples to avoid any disruption of the established organizational hierarchy. In the process, they have bypassed an opportunity to unite business strategy and compensation disciplines in a coalition for enriching the company's performance-management technology.

To move toward a compensation policy wheel with performance at the hub, compensation planners must be a great deal more specific about how strategic and tactical decisions are influenced and actually made within a company. And they must allow this decision structure to dictate the compensation architecture as well as the taxonomy of positions in an organization. Equipped with this base of knowledge, they can then challenge and reshape not only the incentive participation groups but also the grouping of positions for base-salary management, as highlighted in chapter 3. From this point on in the book, the term **performance units** will be used to describe a group of positions, potentially crossing organizational boundaries, whose mission and priorities are identical and whose incentive compensation needs are homogeneous.

Prefab Performance Units

It is not uncommon to find organizations with "built-in" accountability ambiguities resulting from limitations on resources or outright personal accommodations. Consequently, the actual locus and ownership of decisions may be well hidden by a company's table of organization. These obscurities notwithstanding, compensation policymakers are reluctant to venture beyond the beaten path of the published structure when they assemble the building blocks of a new policy; it is safer for them to protect the organization's visible authority network and to ratify policy shortcomings with a tacit surrender to the popular laws of compensation science.

Ask a compensation consultant to describe the logic used to justify incentive eligibility (as Graef S. Crystal does in his treatise *Executive Compensation*), and you will hear a litany of platitudes, each of which sounds compelling but, even by Crystal's own admission, offers little pragmatic guidance:

▌ Labor-intensive service businesses extend incentives deeper than capital-intensive manufacturing enterprises because strategic capital decisions are confined to the corridors of the executive suite, whereas in the service sector, it is important to keep decision making close to the customer.

- Profitable companies tend to spread incentives more liberally than unprofitable concerns, primarily due to the affordability of these incentives.
- Decentralized companies usually include senior division managers in their incentive programs and therefore have a larger eligible group, than comparable centralized companies.

One glimmer of hope is Crystal's plea for a measure of position impact as the criterion for participation. In this scenario, positions with two-way impact (i.e., the ability to both detrimentally *and* beneficially influence company performance) are accorded incentive eligibility, whereas those with only one-way (i.e., detrimental) impact are excluded. As a practical matter, though, a company is more likely to look at its budget and make its own choice between high participation and small rewards, or limited participation and more substantial rewards. This choice, however, is specious in light of the total-compensation principles we examined in the previous chapter. If pay policy is built on a foundation of competitive *total* compensation, then the affordability of incentives for any level in the organization becomes a purely personal question—can the incumbent afford to have compensation at risk?—rather than one of company budgetary significance. To understand this nuance, it is first essential to see how the foregoing rationale for participation group delineation has been put into practice.

The Old Schools

Once a general policy framework for incentive participation is formulated along one of the lines just described, the compensation planner must then define the eligibility cutoff thresholds for the organization. Four widely accepted schools of thought govern the formation of these compensation policy groups. (Little energy will be spent debating the merits of each of these approaches, but the reasons a company might favor one eligibility criterion over another will be briefly examined.)

1. **Salary-Grade School.** Proponents of this school slice the organization horizontally using salary grades as a guide. The validity of this approach depends on the prominence and credibility of a company's salary structure. For example, in large banks or utilities, where positions are identified as much by their salary grade as by their title or function, the salary-grade cutoff is an easily justified guideline for determining incentive eligibility.

2. **Base-Salary School.** As in the salary-grade cutoff approach, the organization is sliced horizontally, but an individual's actual base salary is used as the threshold to define incentive plan eligibility rather than the grade. When actual salary is used, it is typically a sign that the salary structure is nonexistent or that it has fallen into disfavor due to abuse or obsolescence. In the absence of this standard, companies will equate base salary with position impact and align their incentive programs accordingly.

3. **Organizational-Level School.** In this scheme the reporting level of positions, or distance from the CEO on the organization chart, qualifies positions for incentive-plan participation. When incentive eligibility is expected to connote organizational stature as well as provide an additional earnings opportunity, a compensation policy that equates eligibility with organizational level is often preferred. This guideline is also used when neither actual salary nor salary grade is felt to adequately discriminate between the impactful and nonimpactful positions in the organization.

4. **Miscible School.** Companies often combine reporting level with salary-grade cutoffs to define thresholds for incentive-plan participation. Using this type of dual guideline gives the policy planner greater flexibility in applying the criteria selectively and thereby ensuring that no favored positions are arbitrarily excluded from incentive participation due to the constraints imposed by a single criterion. Consequently, if this school's principles are used judiciously, the temptations to cap job evaluations artificially (thereby preventing the entry of borderline positions into the bonus-eligible group), or to cluster salaries just above or below the entry grade, disappear.

Inherent in any of these approaches is the assumption that all jobs in a horizontal band (however defined) are unified by their common performance mission and equal ability to make an imprint on results. Ironically, few compensation planners, and even fewer CEOs, actually believe this far-reaching assumption; and as incentive programs have moved deeper into the organizational hierarchy, its fallacy has become more evident.

Updated Curriculum for the Old Schools

When companies tested their wings with management by objectives (MBO) and other models for performance enhancement, they explored the use of cash bonuses for positions below the senior management level. Chapter 1 pointed to several examples of early broad-based bonus programs that created a payout pool tied to the fortunes of the entire company. When managers gained experience with these programs and recognized that the use of the entire company as a performance unit eroded most of the directional or motivational influence for these employees, they swung the pendulum to the opposite extreme—the narrowest of all performance units, the individual. However, more often than not the administrative costs and subjectivity of individualized performance measures, particularly at lower levels in the organization, were unacceptable.

Undeterred, compensation planners have developed further refinements in recent years that align the scope of the performance unit (i.e., top management, middle management, project team, individual) with the nature of the performance measures (i.e., company financial or special functional objectives). Figure 4.1 schematically illustrates this alignment: At higher levels in the organization, where policy is formulated by a senior management team, heavy emphasis on total company results rather than individual function results is preferred, and there is a bias toward group incentive plans at this level. Conversely, at lower levels in the organization, where accountabilities are more narrowly defined, individual or work-team incentives are used, and these are most typically tied to special functional objectives.

These updates to the old school have not precluded the "mixing and matching" of incentive components. For example, some middle- and senior-management positions may appropriately combine individual and team incentive structures. The individual component would likely be used for the narrower functional objectives, whereas the team incentive would be tied to overall profitability or growth objectives.

In the final analysis, the most beneficial products of this evolution are the acceptance of performance measures that subdivide total corporate performance and the attendant strengthening of the bond between the performance measure and the performance unit. But through all these crusades in search of performance pay's Holy Grail, a critical blaze on the path has been overlooked. Compensation planners have set their sights only along the straight and narrow line of horizontal segmentation when delineating performance units and have typically ignored the intricate relationships that coalesce positions in random patterns across several levels in an organization.

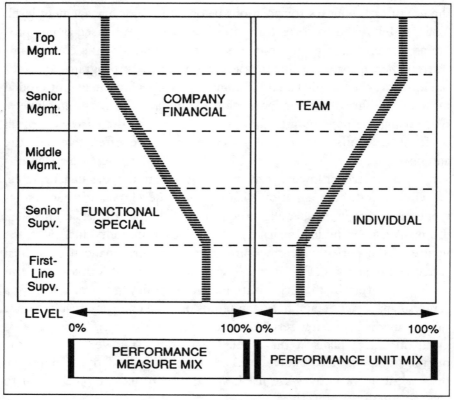

Figure 4.1 Alignment of Performance Units and Measures

The Inner Organization

Managers formulating compensation policy must be willing and able to challenge the sanctity of an organization's reporting structure to bring into clear view the decisive coordinating forces necessary to execute the company's strategy. As many have pointed out, the interesting thing about a corporate organization chart is the blank spaces between the boxes— that's "where the action is." Tables of organization alone seldom reveal how positions must work together to fuse accountabilities that are otherwise segregated according to functional expertise. And compensation planners do not have a distinguished record of penetrating this "inner organization" to congeal these accountabilities. To wit, these planners tend to rely almost exclusively on personal experience or industry peer practices as a rather anemic rationale for the policies they recommend.

Management as well as outside consultants has found it too easy to ignore the critical relationships among business strategy, organization, and compensation. Generally, this convenient verdancy assures the lower-risk profile of promoting conventional and well-tested compensation concepts even if these concepts do not respond to business needs and strategies. Top management and board members similarly may find comfort in the simplicity and familiarity of conventional approaches, and consultants can fall back on their data bases of company practices to support their recommendations.

A vital achievement-pay policy, on the other hand, requires that policy planners create a compelling rationale for performance units that meld the technical-compensation and organizational-analysis disciplines and that have their roots firmly planted in a company's business strategy. Once the policymaker views the organization in this unencumbered light, some new (and some old) cuts at the organization will emerge as natural performance units around which an achievement-pay policy may be constructed.

Vertical Units

When companies explore new avenues for incentive compensation, a natural tendency is for them to cut the organization vertically into separate functional entities. Here again, the sales force emerges as a prototypical example. With a clear mission for top-line revenue results, the sales representatives, two or three layers of sales management, a special (or national) accounts team, and perhaps the customer-service corps are bound together as a single, cohesive compensation policy unit. In the best of circumstances, the sales representatives would have their incentive package split among two or three performance priorities including total sales, a key product introduction, and a national-account support objective; the line managers may be paid for both aggregate and individual subordinate performance; the national-accounts team would focus on account penetration and profitability objectives; and the customer-service function would have incentives tied to service quality indices and productivity.

Another stand-alone function that can be readily segregated from an organization's compensation mainstream is the product development group. Fast on the heels of the "-preneuring" fad, either "entre-" or "intra-", the search for venture management incentives was launched. Recognizing that rewarding the managers for overall corporate performance would hardly be relevant, corporations defined new measures of tracking a venture's progress toward commercial viability. But in light of the uncertainties surrounding most of these new ventures, it was still difficult to assemble an incentive program that could reliably draw managers out of their secure nests within the parent company. Thus, while a great deal of media space has been devoted to new venture-compensation topics, the development of innovative programs for these units has severely lagged behind. (In a later chapter, we will explore practical approaches to this compensation dilemma.)

Manufacturing plants offer yet another obvious opportunity to segregate a functional performance unit. Ever since Frederick W. Taylor installed his first piece-rate pay system, managers have looked for ways to control manufacturing costs by coupling wage rates to a work team's productivity. Today, incentives in the manufacturing environment fall into two broad categories. In the first of these arrangements, the original piece-rate concept has been updated to fit the team or work-cell structure of many current manufacturing operations, but the incentive payouts are still delivered in the form of periodic bonus checks. In the second category, rather than working for an extra paycheck, the plant personnel are tied to a sliding wage scale that moves up or down periodically according to each individual's output relative to a standard.

Because these types of incentive programs have a pronounced effect on the tone of management's relationship with the work force, it is impossible to make universal statements about their applicability or benefit. So, in evaluating the establishment of a manufacturing performance unit, compensation planners should carefully weigh the administrative costs of a program against the anticipated benefits and should further determine whether the individual performance measures can be properly balanced so as not to preempt supervisory priorities or act as surrogate management.

Hybrid Units

When thinking about the inner organization, it is natural to recall the matrix concepts that were introduced in the 1960s to break down organizational barriers within NASA as it was attempting to invigorate its manned space exploration program. Looking back from our present vantage point, we now view matrix organization as an attractive theory for project environments but one that requires a high degree of management sophistication and a strong sense of shared values for its success. Consequently, in name, matrix organization has fallen into disfavor because of its lack of practicability. In reality, however, product- and account-management functions and the newly rediscovered concurrent engineering concept sustain the spirit of the matrix concept by drawing together resources from across an organization's landscape to carry out their mission. And ironically, these consolidated teams can be more complex than their 1960s counterparts, particularly when their members include employees at the same organizational level as well as a vertical mix of employees from different organizational levels.

Companies have recognized that the innovation and quick response they need to capitalize on emerging market opportunities depend on the close interaction of all departments and the willingness of employees to think creatively in their own as well as in other areas. Even without the "glue" of incentive systems to stimulate this cooperation and shared sense of urgency, companies like Ford with its "chimney-breaking" philosophy that dissolves the bureaucratic monoliths in the organization, Honeywell with its cross-functional task teams, and Ameritech with its venture units are just a few examples where hybrid performance units have been formed to eliminate bureaucratic barriers. If a mental paralysis of compensation consultants and their policy-planning counterparts inside companies is allowed to slow the evolution of the compensation discipline while this organization progression takes place, compensation planners will find themselves playing a catch-up game they cannot win.

In Figures 4.2 and 4.3, prototype organizational structures are used to illustrate the hybrid performance-unit concept for distinctly different businesses. The account-management example for a meeting- and conference-planning company assembles a team of functional experts from five different organizational units spanning the life cycle of a program from prospect generation to final billing. Since the organizational structure does not designate an official account "quarterback" with the final authority in setting account-management policies, intramural priorities could easily preempt customer interests in shaping the program-management process. Therefore, an incentive program would fit this situation only if a proper balance could be struck between functional priorities and the quality and profitability of the total program.

In simple terms, this requirement suggests that salespeople must have an abiding concern for the deliverability and profitability of any program they sell; and similarly, the operations and program-estimating people must adopt a marketing perspective that ensures a responsiveness to cus-

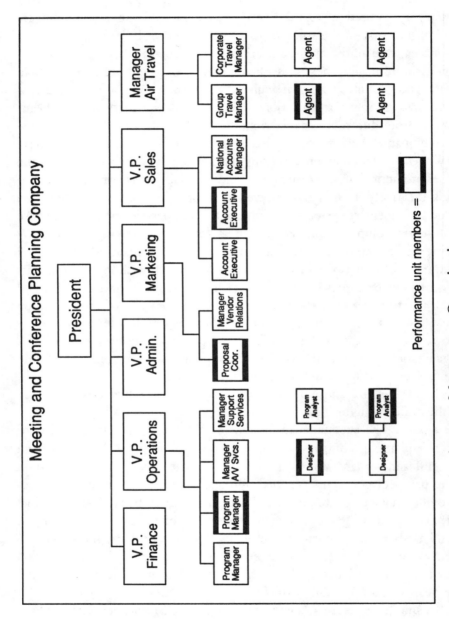

Figure 4.2 Prototype Account-Management Organization

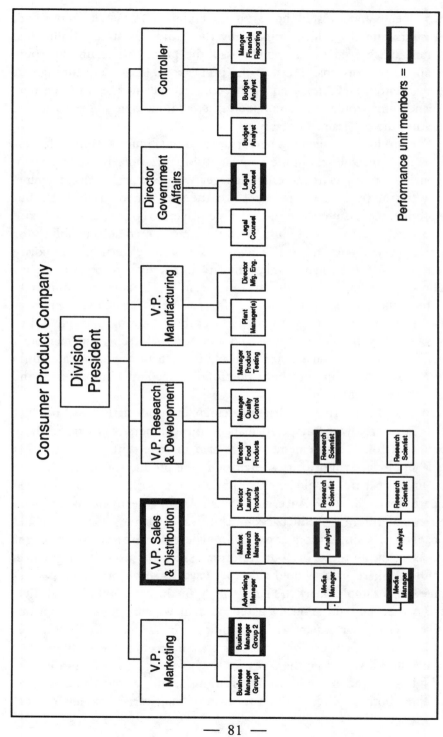

Figure 4.3   Prototype Product-Management Organization

tomers' needs and a vested interest in the company's growth. To this end, an incentive pool could be funded by the profits from each individual program and shared by all members of the performance unit in some predefined proportions. Thus, in the preproposal stages and throughout the negotiation and execution of the contract, all members of the performance unit would have a common interest in completing the sale and operating the program profitably.

The product management performance unit (Figure 4.3) includes positions from three levels in the company's organization. In this scenario, the business manager is the only manager with comprehensive accountability for the product and is, therefore, the undisputed quarterback. But the product team can consist of part-time players who participate in more than a single performance unit. With this fragmented accountability for many team members, there is a high risk that functional-line authority will dominate performance-unit authority in any dispute regarding allocation of time and resources. For an incentive structure to counteract this bias, the at-risk portion of pay for any performance-unit member must be substantial enough to spotlight each competing demand and to motivate the judicious, self-managed allocation of each team member's time. The structure must also be pliable enough to accommodate shifts in the mix of any team member's portfolio of accountabilities during the cycle of the incentive plan.

An incentive structure that creates an internal market in "product shares" that are owned by performance-unit members conforms to these unique portfolio requirements and is also in tune with the competing short- and long-term priorities intrinsic in the product-management process. Product shares would be either purchased by, or granted or optioned to, participants in accordance with their roles in a performance unit and their mix of different product accountabilities. (A business manager would probably have a single product portfolio, whereas a research analyst might have as many as three or four different issues of product shares in a portfolio.) Share price would ride the waves of each product's performance (for example, market share, sales growth, profitability), and dividends would be paid annually based on achievement of predefined objectives. As any participant's responsibilities change, or if the participant is moved into a new position, the current "market" value of his or her product shares would be the basis for any exchange or redemption.

Neither of the examples outlined in this section is mechanically simple. They both require, through the use of multivariate models of performance, the accretion of value—program-based in the first scenario, and product-based in the second. But executives of these types of companies readily understand that managing performance in these environments requires an intricate mix of perspectives and decision-making skills. Ignoring this critical alignment of performance-unit composition and performance-measurement criteria by relying on the conventional horizontal layering of incentive programs will inevitably lead to counterproductive behavior among the managers in these hybrid units. Compensation planners should therefore be wary that "off-the-shelf" answers to these difficult questions may break down the very interactive linkages that the hybrid structures are intended to create.

Outlier Units

With the framework established thus far, positions directly related to the strategic core of a business can be accommodated with one of the three taxonomies described (that is, the old horizontal school, the vertical, and the hybrid alternatives just examined). Many outlying positions will inevitably be cast in supporting roles to several performance units instead of being assigned exclusively to a single unit. Human resources, financial accounting, data processing, facilities management, and shared manufacturing management personnel are examples of positions that frequently fall into this performance unit no-man's land.

But is it fair to exclude these positions from any incentive opportunity? Most companies, implicitly rejecting a total-compensation model (that could maintain compensation equity by increasing the guaranteed portion of pay for these positions), decide that exclusion is unacceptable. Though there are specific conditions (related to the company's stage in its life cycle, examined in chapter 7) that support the inclusion of these positions in the programs, there are also significant drawbacks inherent in their misapplication.

Recalling an earlier discussion, companies commonly include the senior managers of outlier functions in the top management performance unit. This policy is usually explained by the proximity of these positions to the policy inner sanctum and by the affordability of at-risk pay for the senior managers. Below this level, however, where influence on either policy or results is filtered through a complex network of authorities and organization layers, the achievement-pay premise disintegrates. Pay leverage in the absence of perceived influence will in bad times be viewed only as an insidious form of game-playing and in good times as merely a base-salary deferral technique.

Forging a New Taxonomy

Compensation planners, as a separate species, resemble the four-year-old lemmings who, overwhelmed by their native instincts, leap from high cliffs to their demise. The planners seem to blindly follow their instincts when they proffer a menu of policy alternatives that are nothing but the soft diet of their discipline. In so doing, they are writing an epitaph that merely confirms the business world's sharpening criticism of pay for performance and denies the planners' contribution to their companies' performance management process.

If outside consultants are involved in policy formulation, their usual first step is to develop their own perspective on business needs. Therefore, to provide a backdrop for their policy recommendations, consultants will interview a cross-section of managers as a precursor to defining key success factors, reworking mission statements, and assessing organizational values. But this process is often nothing more than an analytical smoke screen whose outcome bears no resemblance to the realities of the business. The reader may choose one of several explanations for these recurring phenomena. Perhaps the risk of untested concepts is perceived as too great; or maybe the administrative complexity of more-sophisticated programs is overwhelming; or the planners may be unskilled in the disciplines required to blend business analysis, organization design, and compensation policy.

For whatever reason, the reluctance to pursue an integrated view of these policy issues has led to a rationalization that compensation and organization are specialized, unconnected business disciplines. Witness the common practice of human resources departments structured with a stand-alone compensation function that is separate from organization planning and that is rarely asked to provide counsel on organizational issues. Consulting firms similarly offer specialty organization and strategy, or compensation and benefits, services to mirror their clients' philosophies. But this bifurcated view of the problem-solving process can never fully address the complexities of resolving organizational and compensation issues in an integrated fashion and will therefore fail to forge any innovative performance-unit taxonomy. To respond to this dilemma, an analytical discipline must be found that reduces the reliance of policymakers on intuitive conclusions and that places political power structures in the background. Furthermore, this new discipline must not be shackled by the encumbrances of conventional practice and must encourage policy formulation that openly challenges enshrined assumptions about business strategy and decision authorities.

Uncovering Performance Management Imperatives

Practitioners in the compensation-planning discipline are becoming adept at presenting a facade that suggests they have incisive knowledge about how compensation, organization, and strategy fit together. The planners are no longer satisfied with their image as mere researchers and are striving to assume a new persona as business analysts who ask penetrating questions about strategy and the management process. As facades go, however, this one is particularly deceptive in that the mound of business information that is collected rarely exerts perceptible influence on compensation-program design. As has been our purpose throughout this book, with the analytical model developed in the following paragraphs we wish to bring subterfuge of this ilk out into the open and force explicit examination of the very linkages that are implied by the policy planner's purported role.

This analytical model is designed to help the planner and management complete the compensation connections and to stimulate a thoughtful reassessment of policy assumptions. It is split into three progressive stages: environmental intelligence gathering, management-hypothesis testing, and performance-unit design. The common thread that runs through all of these stages is a reliance on strategy—to reveal the company's approach to the marketplace and to create a rationale for changing compensation policy. Internal compensation planners do not aggressively pursue their nascent role as organizational or competitive-strategy experts, and large human resources consulting firms either have a separate division specializing in this discipline or abdicate these issues to other firms like McKinsey & Company or The Boston Consulting Group. Yet it is hard to imagine how management can expect compensation to contribute meaningfully to the performance-management art if compensation planners lack a working knowledge of business strategy (and its crucial underlying assumptions) and are incapable of shaping performance units in accordance with that strategy.

Business strategy is by its very nature a foundation of constancy upon which the entire portfolio of business policies is constructed. In stark contrast, compensation policy has most often been considered little more than a high-level payroll-administration procedure anchored in the data base of industry pay practices. For achievement pay to become a vital reality, however, compensation policy must tack to a business strategy anchorage. Michael Porter in *Competitive Strategy* states that a "strategy being followed by a business must reflect assumptions management is making about its industry and the business's relative position in the industry." Thus, these assumptions are the essence of strategy, and they are the key to the compensation planner's understanding of performance management.

How can the compensation planner, from the insulated confines of a human resources department, discover this essence? First, the planner must know where to look, and Porter's model of competitive strategy formulation (somewhat reconstituted in Figure 4.4) provides a useful map. Assumptions about the company's strengths and weaknesses, the market opportunities (from both the customers' and competitors' perspectives), and the chemistry of the management team combine to shape what the business has to do to meet its strategic objectives and to exploit its market opportunities.

Next, the planner needs to develop an explicit profile of the most important competitive dimensions for the business (for example, the pricing/profitability dynamics, capital-allocation decision criteria, product-development initiatives, service-quality issues, management competence and style) to understand how the company is managing these key facets of performance. Figure 4.5 outlines a series of topics that the planner can address with senior managers to help develop this profile. Through an exploration of these topics, a compensation planner should become intimately familiar with the company's approach to the market and its competitive posture. And above all, the planner should form impressions about what role compensation can play in complementing the strategy and what organizational or management practices may impede strategy execution.

Armed with this base of information, the planner is now ready to challenge the implicit or explicit axioms that currently shape the company's performance-management approach. When the planner discovers gaps between the existing management practices and the stated business objectives, the underlying premise for compensation policy change emerges in the form of *performance management hypotheses*. Those hypotheses present a contrasting view of the managerial focal points and

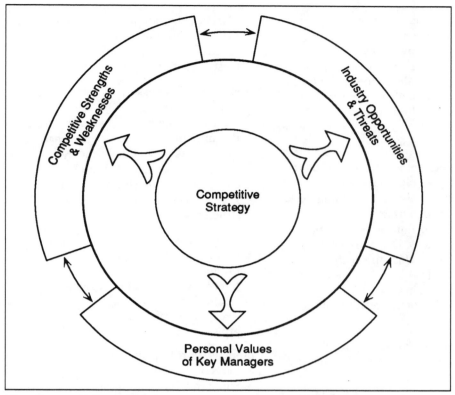

Figure 4.4 Competitive Strategy Formulation Model
Adapted from Michael E. Porter, *Competitive Strategy*. Original model is somewhat more complex and includes one additional dimension, "societal expectations," which has less applicability for this discussion.

are used as a foil to build management consensus on the behavioral changes required to improve strategy execution. Usually, these behavioral changes involve either a modification of working relationships or a shift in priorities, and they can be approached from three different angles. The most radical is a realignment of the organization's reporting structure; the less radical alternatives include the definition of new individual and group performance measures and the reconfiguration of compensation performance units.

Throughout this process, the compensation planner, though not directly impugning the company's strategy or its objectives, will certainly be shining a harsh spotlight on the company's raison d'être. But the planner must take this aggressive stance, because compensation policy is an unavoidable bridge between individual manager behavior and strategy

Products/Markets:
- Economic sensitivity
- Growth characteristics
- Customer concentration
- Product mix concentration
- Distribution channel mix and dominance
- New business development cycle/process

Technology/Resource Base:
- Capital intensity
- Investment planning cycle
- Investment mix (maintenance/growth)
- R & D requirements
- Product life span
- Labor environment (type, supply)
- Supplier relationships

Competition:
- Market-share profile
- Competitor strengths and weaknesses
- Competitive barriers
- Competitive advantages
- Type of competition (price, service, quality)

Management Focus:
- Cash flow
- Return on investment
- Revenue growth

- Market penetration/diversification
- Product diversification/innovation
- Profits/earnings per share
- Cost reduction/productivity

Management Processes:
- Capital budgeting
- Annual planning and objective setting
- Planning history and variance analysis
- Manager skills and deficiencies
- Style (collegial vs. autocratic)
- Customer-relationship management
- Policy formulation and decision structures

Planning Focus:
- By function (short- and long-term)
- Products/markets
- Internal vs. external development
- Key milestones
- Recognition of trade-offs (e.g., growth/profitability)

Compensation Impact:
- Perceived equity
- Support of planning process
- Prominence of compensation in management processes
- Risk/reward philosophy
- Personal compensation objectives

Figure 4.5 Business Topics for Compensation-Policy Analysis

execution. To believe otherwise is to confirm the evisceration of a company's achievement-pay convictions.

Where "Performance at the Hub" Begins: A Case Example

A large national market-research firm was suffering from sluggish growth and stagnant profitability. The CEO was convinced that weaknesses in the existing discretionary incentive plan, which was designed for the senior managers, were an important contributor to this performance malaise. An outside consultant was called in to develop new incentive programs for the account executives, the office of the chairman, and key operations managers.

As a first step, the consultant spent three or four hours working with the firm's top management to develop an overview of the company's objectives and competitive strategy. With this step behind them, they were now prepared to probe, through interviews with account and operations managers across the organization, how these strategies were reflected in the day-to-day management practices.

The table in Figure 4.6 combines the results of this interviewing process with the format prescribed in Figure 4.5. When these analytical components were juxtaposed, a logical flow was created that allowed the consultant to compare, in the context of the business attributes, the stated strategy to the tangible evidence of operating methods and management processes. The primary purpose of this exercise, however, was not just to provide a mirror into which management could look for an eyeful of self-discovery. Though this purpose could be beneficial, the consultant's success depended on a broader purview—that of exploring the validity of the company's performance-management practices in the context of its strategy and the unalterable characteristics of the business. The company's stated strategy was quite simple—to be the lowest-cost "producer" of the commodity-oriented data-collection and tabulation services and to distinguish itself in the market by providing "value-added" counsel on marketing strategy.

Some insightful findings from this analysis included the following:

■ Technical support staff, dedicated to account groups and prohibited from crossing their boundaries, were suffering from poor utilization and personal development neglect.

Business Attribute Screen	Findings	Current Management Approach
Products/Markets	Stable base of customers creates relatively low revenue concentration Contract specifications are dictated by customer Business development cycle requires up to one year Customer buying influences are fragmented Growth in customer base and revenues is slow New technology eroding available market	Focus on account penetration and profitability improvement Selective investment in product development Separated project specification and costing accountabilities Reactive "opportunity" selling
Technology/Resource base	Proven data-collection facilities, data control, and state-of-the-art tabulation capabilities required to be competitive Cost structure is major determinant of competitive advantage New technology requires high-cost/high-risk investment	Limited investment in high-return cost-reduction programs and equipment Optimal use of contract services
Competition	Services are undifferentiated from competitive offerings in customers' perception; primary distinguishing feature is expertise of lead account executive	Quality standards set by customers Focus on price competition for new business Creation of transfer-cost barriers to competition on repeat projects

Management focus	Individual project profitability is the primary building block of company financial welfare; accountability for revenue growth or profitability improvement is fragmented	Account-profitability-management responsibility assigned to account managers
Management process	Management control systems are well entrenched Execution of projects supersedes most business-development efforts with existing customers Absence of an account planning discipline High degree of account executive autonomy and provincialism	Account manager autonomy and dedicated account team resources Fragmented management of execution modules Account manager/customer continuity creates cellular account authority Functionization of project execution (operations) resources
Planning focus	Three distinct and competing visions of company's future without reconciliation	Annual margin-improvement initiatives Maintenance of technology status quo
Compensation impact	Connection between compensation (incentives) and performance is ambiguous Distribution of incentives is highly discretionary Bonus practices create privileged "caste" that excludes many key contributors	Senior management gainsharing

Figure 4.6 Aligning Business Attributes with Management Processes

■ Project execution was split into several steps, but no operations expert assumed total accountability for project execution or cost and quality control.

■ Developing technology threatened to accelerate the erosion of the company's traditional market, but no accountability had been assigned for long-range planning and technology assessment.

■ Protection and development of existing account relationships was the short-term imperative for profitability, but incentives did not explicitly focus on account-revenue growth.

Though these observations may sound organizational in character, further reflection reveals a relevance to compensation that is inextricable. They indicate what organizational barriers must be removed to allow management to pursue the company's strategy; they suggest how different components of the organization must work together as a performance unit to manage critical activities; and they clearly intimate measures of achievement that can sharpen management's focus on the needs of the business. The results of the consultant's interview analysis are summarized in Figure 4.7. In this table, the current management approach is compared to an alternative view—management hypotheses formulated as a direct product of the environmental analysis but presupposing none of the sacred cows of past management practice. The business rationale for each counterpoint is perhaps the most important element of the analysis thus far, for it creates the premise for change in terms that all managers can understand and view objectively—namely, the welfare of the business itself.

Having reached an accord with management on these hypotheses, the consultant now had to consider the organizational and performance-management implications of the findings (Figure 4.8). But before delving into these conclusions, note that through all of this discussion, not a word has been spoken about the mechanical structure of a compensation program. The primary focus has been on *what* to pay for and *who* should be held accountable. The fact is that compensation planners, whether internal or external, cannot add much value if their scope is limited to a narrow mechanical focus. And for the price that is paid in consulting fees, internal resource time, and organizational disruption, much more should be expected.

For this market-research firm, substantial organizational change was needed—the shifting of resources from dedicated account groups to centralized project-execution teams specializing in particular types of proj-

Current Management Approach	Alternative Management Hypotheses	Rationale
Products/Markets:		
Account penetration/profitability	Dedicated new-account acquisition	Must aggressively seek new accounts
Selective product investment	Account-penetration imperatives	and protect exisiting relationships to
Separated specification/costing	Use of technology enhancements to	shore up position in shrinking market
Reactive selling	secure key customers	
	Integration of key operations and	
	account-management accountabilities	
Technology/Resource base:		
Limited investment in cost-reduction	Upgraded analytical/consulting skills	Cost of major new technologies too
initiatives	Investment commitment to state-of-the-	high-tab technology is core business
Optimal use of contract services	art data-tabulation technologies	Higher margin to be gained from value-
		added consulting services
Competition:		
Customer quality standards	Higher visibility of account manager	Consistent client value requires uniform
Price competition	throughout project	quality/cost standards
Technology transfer-cost barriers	Assertion of uniform *company* quality/	Lead account executive is key to client's
	cost standards with customers	perception of value added
Management focus:		
Account profitability focus	Project profitability	Must be able to analyze and explain
	Account group margin contribution	aggregate profitability variances at the
	Account penetration	individual project level
		Much business "left on the table" by
		account managers

(continued)

Figure 4.7 Formulating Management Hypotheses

Current Management Approach	Alternative Management Hypotheses	Rationale
		Need to reposition account manager as research planning resource for customer
Management processes: Account-manager autonomy/customer continuity Dedicated account-team resources Project-execution fragmentation	Creation of support-staff pools Regular rotation of staff personnel Specialization of execution resources by type of project (rather than by project process) Dual visibility (manager/supervisor) at accounts	Concentration of accountability and improvement of project control Breaking down cellular insulation of account teams Improved utilization of support-staff resources Strengthened account relationships
Planning focus: Margin improvement initiatives Technology status quo	Account-penetration (new projects) staff development	Need to capitalize on business base Need to strengthen/broaden skills of research staff
Compensation impact: Senior management gainsharing	Account-group planning and objective setting tied to incentive payouts Concentration on growth: • Revenues per account • Staff skill bench marks and cross-utilization • New accounts	Survival in shrinking market requires increased share and high staff productivity

Figure 4.7 (Continued)

	Implications		
Management Hypotheses	Organization Structure	Performance Unit	Performance Measure
Management focus: Project profitability Account-group margin contribution Account penetration			Dual accountability for project and account profitability Account-growth objectives
Management processes: Support-staff pools Staff rotation Project "type" staff specialization Dual customer visibility	Segregation of project-management and utility-service functions within operations department	Creation of project-type "business units"	Project-type "business unit" accounting and unified product accountability
Planning focus: Account penetration Staff development	Creation of career paths and human-resources–planning council	Long-range-planning unit made up of top management and senior account managers	Staff development bench marks Long-range stock value appreciation
Compensation impact: Account-group incentives tied to objectives Concentration on growth	Consolidated accountability for operations; elimination of dedicated account-group resources	Dual membership of account managers in account-group and top-management performance units	Account-revenue growth and profitability

(continued)

Figure 4.8 Organizational and Performance-Management Implications

Management Hypotheses	Implications		
	Organization Structure	Performance Unit	Performance Measure
Products/Markets: Dedicated new-account acquisition Account-penetration imperatives Technology enhancements Account management/ operations integration	Product-development council created for long-range development and technology planning Restructuring of operations into project-type groups with dedicated account-manager liaison	Creation of new business-development team with specific targets Creation of formal project-execution teams	Existing account-growth goals for account managers Project budgetary and write-off tracking
Technology/Resource base: Upgraded consulting skills of account managers State-of-the-art data tabulation	Technology-planning counsel		Accountability for portion of technical-support-staff budget allocated to account managers Establishment of report-quality standards and review board
Competition: Higher account-manager visibility with customer Uniform quality/cost standards	Project-type organization of operations function		Standards for customer calls and presentation of final reports

Figure 4.8 *(Continued)*

ects. A reshaping of performance units, independent of the organizational change, was also necessary to intensify the new business–development effort and sharpen the product-management focus of the business. A planning discipline for the account executives, coupled to objective-based account-revenue growth and profitability incentives, was necessary to protect the short-term welfare and earnings of the firm. And finally, a long-range-planning performance unit with a special stock-purchase arrangement must be held accountable for two essential ingredients of the company's future: staff development and technological investments.

It would be natural for an internal compensation planner to dismiss this methodical analysis as unnecessary and merely the product of an outside consultant's need to build credibility by gaining familiarity with the company. This premise is true, however, only if the compensation planner can articulate the performance-management counterpoints at the onset without doing an analysis. These counterpoints underlie management's discomfort with existing compensation policy, and they foretell the changes in management behavior that are desired. So it should be evident that compensation cannot "fix" organizational problems and that it is crucial to separate organizational and compensation solutions to management problems in order to control the expectations and to manage the implementation of any change in compensation policy.

5

Pay Risk

Impact beyond Equity

Our principal aim in this chapter is to create a calculus of pay risk that puts "teeth" in a company's achievement-pay philosophy by cross-matching job characteristics to compensation mix. In the previous two chapters, the boundaries of pay risk have been stretched beyond their salary and organizational strictures. But as yet this book has not prescribed a formula for establishing a specific position's compensation mix; nor has this issue been addressed rigorously within the tenets of existing compensation technology, except as a timeworn competitive research topic.

According to a 1989 survey by Hewitt Associates, a large benefits and compensation consultant, bonuses and long-term incentives (that is, stock programs) make up half of total pay for top managers. Annual bonuses are typically 50 percent of base salary for these managers, and annualized long-term incentives are worth almost as much as base salary. If these figures are compared with similar data for 1982, it is readily apparent that the total compensation of these executives has been on a steep climb. Substantial increases in variable pay, not only in absolute terms but also as a proportion of total pay, can be noted, and during this same period (1982–1989), base-salary levels were reported to rise by 49 percent. This acceleration in total compensation might be plausible if similar gains in corporate performance had also been realized. But in reality, all evidence suggests that this correlation is absent, and perhaps executives have learned the same lesson as Huck Finn, who said, "What's the use you learning to do right when it's troublesome to do right and ain't no trouble to do wrong and the wages is just the same?" Thus, the run-up in what is touted as high-risk pay is arguably nothing more than the sophistry of stockholder relations.

Uncertainty of receipt is the quintessential nature of pay risk. It is not merely the arithmetic result of subtracting base salary from total compensation; instead, it is measured by the probability of achieving any given result within an incentive performance range. In Figure 5.1, an incentive payout function is charted to illustrate how real pay risk might be varied depending on the structure of an incentive plan.

The vertical axis of the graph represents the probability of achieving a particular performance level within the payout range, represented by the horizontal axis. According to this graph, a significant segment of the payout range, between performance thresholds 1 and 2, is virtually guaranteed. In practice, this could occur if an incentive plan is structured to yield an incentive payout above a threshold of earnings, say $5 million, when the unit's performance has exceeded $10 million in each of the past three years, and no major change in business conditions is anticipated.

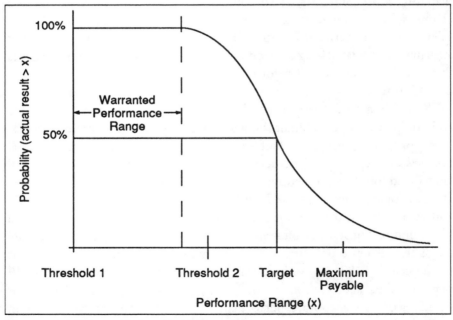

Figure 5.1 Determining Real Pay Risk

The probability for achieving results above threshold 2 drops off dramatically and continues to decrease through the target range and up to the maximum payable threshold, where the probability is less than 5 percent.

Though small incentive payments between thresholds 1 and 2 can enhance the motivational value of a program and do not necessarily circumvent the purpose of at-risk pay, significant payments in this range will usually adulterate the motivational effect by creating compensation policy's version of diminishing returns. If, for example, Paul Fireman at Reebok earned $12 million of his $14 million in "executive commissions" in the low- or no-risk portion of the performance range, stockholders should not be surprised if his "kick to the finish" for the next $2 million lacks crazed dedication. Although the exorbitant pay packages of Fireman and his kindred celebrity CEOs attract a lot of media attention and criticism, the tumescence of incentive pay for senior management is widespread and in many cases is just as deceptively gratuitous as these high-profile examples. Compensation planners must therefore be on guard to ensure that incentive plans properly align the payout for any result with the degree of difficulty of achieving the result so that the motivational equation is always in balance.

The Research Illusion

Compensation surveys, either published or proprietary, are the oracular voice in guiding variable-compensation policy. Base-salary and total-compensation data are almost always included in these surveys to presumably show how leverage in pay plans is used within and across industry groups. Mark Twain's oft-quoted observation that "there are lies, damn lies, and statistics" finds an easy mark in the published variable-pay data, since these data are consistently unreliable as indicators of either individual company variable-pay policies or the actual amount of variable pay earned by an executive.

These surveys usually provide two sets of data: averages and quartiles of base salary, and similar statistics for total annual cash compensation. Occasionally, further description of bonus practices will present bonus averages expressed as a percentage of base salary for each surveyed position. Unfortunately, these data are typically misleading and do not allow the compensation planner to pinpoint the actual **or** target bonus payment amounts. This evidence is obfuscated by several common data-collection and presentation practices:

■ Many surveys mix the findings from bonus-paying and non-bonus-paying companies, thereby, at least in theory, increasing base salaries, reducing total compensation levels, and compressing the at-risk pay gap.

■ Even if surveys segregate data of bonus-paying and non-bonus-paying companies, the simple difference between total compensation and base salary will not always give the true picture of *targeted* compensation mix. Since these data reflect actual earnings, they will naturally rise and fall with both individual and company performance (depending on the structure of the incentive programs) and will therefore disguise this key statistic. In addition, policy planners should be wary of surveys that report bonus percentage levels, since these again are based on actual payouts rather than targets.

■ The total amount of pay exceeding base salary is not always at risk. Thus, as we noted in this chapter's introduction, even if the shortcomings in the data base cited previously are overcome, planners should still be circumspect in their use of surveys to set compensation-mix policy.

These statistical weaknesses (at least the first two) have not escaped the attention of most policy planners, and in turn the planners are reluctant to use survey data explicitly to support variable-compensation recommendations. But, lacking any other compelling rationale for compensation mix, they will draw broad correlations between company size and organizational reporting level and fall back on the familiar, "trusty" horizontal slicing of the organization to set the variable-pay targets.

To their line-management constituency, this latitudinal approach is often appealing. First, it can be easily communicated as a promotion or recognition program. With bonus eligibility thresholds tied to a position's organizational stature, managers will typically view their bonus-plan participation as a signal that they have "arrived" at a certain level of membership in the company's inner circle. Second, if all positions at the same level are assigned identical bonus targets, promotions or reassignments are not impeded by differing variable-compensation amounts. As noted in chapter 3, divergence from this regular "stacking" of incentive programs can cause base-salary inversions or exaggerated salary progressions along natural career paths, if high-incentive-mix jobs feed lower-mix jobs or vice versa. (A career-mapping solution to this dilemma that requires some additional organizational analysis was illustrated in Figure 3.8.) Adopting the more conventional pattern, however, assures that laterally reassigned positions will have the same bonus target amount and that both the fixed and the variable components of compensation will be increased for promoted managers.

If the compensation planner is seduced by these appeals and treats mix policy as a research and administrative exercise, an illusion of compensation equity will be created, while an important kinship with job analysis and organization design is denied. The planner should be aware that this is not an insignificant trade-off, since pay risk is the most unalloyed means of communicating an individual position's accountability, and is thus the very core of achievement pay. To unwittingly impose rules of latitudinal symmetry on an organization whose strategic instincts compel assymmetry is to blatantly compromise achievement pay's guiding principles.

A License for Individual Initiative

When comparing positions at any given organizational level, one inevitably finds that the positions are not endowed with equal freedom to take action and that their direct impact on results varies significantly. The job of matching compensation programs and at-risk pay amounts to these widely varying position characteristics is a fundamental responsibility of the compensation planner. Before we delve into a method for making these matches, though, it is worthwhile to pause briefly and reflect on the purposes of at-risk pay.

The financial purposes of at-risk pay are easily discerned. Leveraging the cost of a group of employees to the financial welfare of a company is a valid compensation strategy, but if this leveraging principle is placed at the hub of the compensation-policy wheel, it is unlikely that both the *financial* and *behavioral* purposes of at-risk pay can coexist. A focus on financial leverage usually precludes a diligent search for the mission accountability networks and therefore will only accidentally yield a match of position authority and attendant demands for individual initiative with appropriate levels of compensation risk. Moreover, if this leverage is at the hub, the selection of performance measures is most often driven by communication efficiency rather than by individual position accountability, dissipating the value of incentive pay as a directional force. So before the compensation planner makes any decisions about compensation risk, the question of purpose must be faced as a stark contrast.

Suppose communication efficiency and administrative simplicity persistently arise as an organization's acid tests for program acceptability. Then, even if management eulogizes employees as "our company's most valuable assets," this "Nospeak" should not mislead the planner to ignore the palpable truth—that employees are not regarded as assets but rather as an expense item to be leveraged to the greatest extent possible. If, on the other hand, management centers on the organization's need for leadership and initiative and for channeling employees' energy toward the crucial priorities of the business, then the compensation planner can be reasonably assured of management's intent to place performance at the hub and to use incentives for their behavioral purposes.

The planner should also be aware that management intent will become murky as concrete compensation programs emerge from conceptual specifications. The unfamiliarity and intricacy of these programs may pose the first hurdle; and additional, perhaps more challenging, hurdles will arise as management is forced to make deeper commitments to specific direction (performance measures) and objectives (incentive targets). These commitments threaten management's flexibility and, when coupled to true pay risk, also portend a clear trade-off between management's control and individual employees' initiative. Confronted with these obstacles, compensation planners will meet face to face for the first time the peril of their purpose. They must resolutely present the full range of management's choices and demonstrate the sacrifices inherent in any dilution of the original specifications. Wavering at this juncture will have long-term consequences, leading to the planner's loss of policy-level credibility and the company's loss of an opportunity to incrementally advance its compensation art.

Consider a large national soft-drink manufacturer whose product lines, markets, and distribution channels are well established and whose long-range strategy narrowly restricts product or market diversification. In fact, there is a significant risk that any new product introduction will "cannibalize" existing products rather than take share from competitors' products. Most marketing decisions in this company are made by a top-management policy committee, and any initiatives for product acquisition or development are prompted by this committee. As might be expected, day-to-day decisions regarding local distribution, pricing, and customer service are thoroughly routinized and are subject to exception only by senior field management. In this environment, it would be hard for a compensation planner to argue for a high-risk incentive plan that encouraged an assertive management style and independent initiative at any level below that of senior management. (It should be readily apparent to the reader at this point that if the truck drivers on the retail routes earn case commissions, only a nominal amount of their pay is truly at risk.)

A regional manufacturer/distributor of millwork building products offers a striking counterexample to the national soft drink corporation. This company's product portfolio includes a broad range of standard door and window products as well as many custom moldings, stair parts, and fireplace treatments. Though regional in scope, each market served is influenced not only by national financial and home-building market trends, but also by very localized weather and economic conditions. The company is organized by branches, each with warehouse, sales and distribution capabilities, and its success depends on each unit's ability to react quickly to local competitive pressures and to adjust product and service mix to fit the particular demands of its customers. In this setting, if the initiative, creativity, and responsiveness of the branch management team were blunted by corporate bureaucracy, the branch would consistently undermine its credibility with customers. Consequently, a high-risk incentive plan that firmly affixes accountability for branch performance to the branch sales, customer service, and general managers is a competitive necessity.

As these two examples demonstrate, pay risk can be thought of as a regulator that governs the intensity of a manager's participation in decision processes and his or her willingness to take independent action. We realize that in these turbulent times of budget cutting and merger- and acquisition-induced staff reductions, the introduction of greater uncertainty through leveraged compensation may be perceived as incongruous. In fact, as we noted earlier, there is ample evidence that many companies opt for the safe harbor of reduced pay risk to soften the blow of eroding job security. Quick to point out trends of this nature, the business press is already headlining the growing mass of workers who are unnerved by job security concerns and are forming a risk-averse cult with an ideology that says, "Keep your head down and don't make waves." But a low-risk compensation program does not come without a price. Putting aside the attendant increase in fixed compensation costs, the potential loss in management initiative and assertiveness may be a far more costly consequence of this low-risk pay strategy.

Above all, a too-conservative cultural direction is at odds with a more conspicuous and durable need. The innovative and aggressive management style required to recapture American industry's leadership in the intensely competitive global marketplace cannot be nurtured in a low-risk climate. Thus, management is confronted with a clear choice: React to the short-term trauma by applying the salve of an income-security safety net, or recognize the myopia of such a strategy and start today to inculcate a new credo that tolerates dissent, encourages intellectual risk, and forgives miscalculations in the interest of creativity.

Job Evaluation's Third Dimension

If pay risk is to be matched with position impact and accountability, bonus participation criteria for contrasting positions like the controller and the senior sales and marketing executive must be redefined. A third dimension of job evaluation (appended to the familiar dimensions of knowledge and accountability that are incorporated in most evaluation models) can serve as a consistent framework for aligning job characteristics with compensation mix. This new dimension (illustrated in Figure 5.2) focuses on the interaction of environment- and job-dependent criteria that circumscribe a position's fitness for at-risk pay.

The environmental criteria, forming the outer ring of the model, can guide the compensation planner in evaluating the context of management's decision making. Understanding the pressures on the organization's competencies emanating from external change, competitive antagonism, and growth-induced stress will systematically lead the compensation planner to develop a firm rationale for setting the overall level of risk in a company's payroll. Yet this environmental assessment provides only a relative sense of high, medium, or low risk for a company, and it must be combined with the impact and accountability factors at the core of the model to determine the pay risk for individual positions.

Taken one at a time, the environmental criteria have distinct implications for the compensation-risk profile of a company; together, however, their effect is multiplicative rather than additive. For example, the impact of market stability on the risk profile can directly modify the effect of the competitive climate on this profile, and vice versa. To understand these concepts more fully, though, it is necessary to explore their definition and application individually:

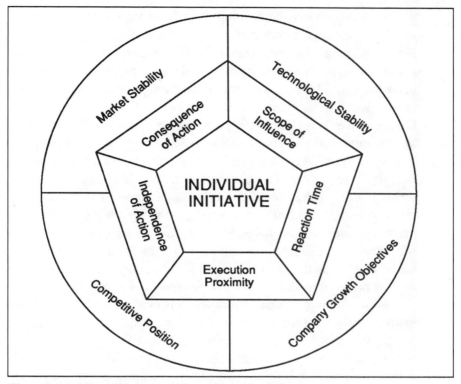

Figure 5.2 The Compensation-Risk Equation

▌ **Market Stability.** In dynamic markets where demand is growing rapidly, new segments are emerging, and the competitive variables are constantly shifting, an aggressive, risk-oriented management team that is always seeking and responding quickly to opportunities for competitive advantage is usually desirable. On the other hand, in more stable markets where the competitive players have attained a state of equilibrium, individual initiative and independent action can be more damaging than beneficial, and a risk-oriented management team could be a liability to the company.

▌ **Technological Stability.** Companies competing in industries that require a steady stream of new products and/or manufacturing techniques must have an aggressive management team that is able to set a course for the long-term and that is willing to take calculated risks and champion personal commercial causes. In more sedate technological environments, such aggressive action may prove to be more costly than productive; company resources may be diverted and market position and earnings sacrificed for the sake of a manager's professional career goals. To ensure that false signals are not sent throughout the organization, compensation programs in these instances normally should have a low-risk profile, and management behavior should be heavily influenced by policies, controls, and predefined tactical plans.

▌**Competitive Position.** The competitive climate of a company should influence the compensation-risk policy by modulating the impact of the market and technological stability considerations. An industry leader, even if confronted with volatile markets and rapid technological change, is likely to be more cautious in its decision making than a "wildcat" company aggressively trying to enter the market or increase its share. The industry leader can patiently observe from the sidelines the initiatives of the wildcat, feeling confident that it has the marketing and technical muscle to respond to any breakthroughs that might disrupt the market equilibrium.

A good example of this phenomenon is evident in the office- and institutional-furniture industry. Steelcase, Inc., a Grand Rapids, Michigan, manufacturer and distributor, had for many years sustained a dominant position in this industry, but in the early 1970s it was confronted with the open-office concept pioneered by Herman Miller, Inc. Such a radical departure from conventional permanent-wall office design was a clear threat to Steelcase's leadership, but during the launch period of this product it maintained a wait-and-see attitude. As this new product gained acceptance, however, Steelcase was quick to respond with its own modular furniture line and was able to recapture and surpass its earlier dominant share position. Though the two companies were vying head-to-head for market share, the competitive climate at Steelcase pointed to a compensation program that did not encourage a high degree of individual initiative; whereas at Herman Miller, the company's viability depended on an aggressive, risk-taking management team during the crucial product-development and launch stages.

▌**Company Growth Objectives.** Today's business sages predict that internal growth will supplant acquired growth in the 1990s. In response, the growth-oriented CEO must nurture the innovator, the creative thinker—the manager who has opinions and is not reluctant to voice them. Given these organizational attributes of growth, compensation programs can assume a high-risk profile and complement a company's objectives, or they can become a constant source of frustration for the CEO who tries to squeeze product, service, and marketing innovations from a risk-averse management team. If, conversely, a company opts for a slow-growth, market-protection strategy, high-risk compensation programs could pose similar frustrations for the management team by paying for individual initiative in an environment that is by design bureaucratic.

Before we move on to a discussion of the evaluation factors in the inner core of the model, it is worthwhile to revisit an earlier premise—that the environmental traits should not be viewed independently, but rather as highly interactive influences on a company's compensation-policy response to its markets. At first glance, it may seem that technological stability and market stability are not necessarily linked. But many markets that show a significant degree of instability (for example, commercial printing, farm implements) have a technological base that is relatively stable (nobody has found a practical alternative to offset or rotogravure for high-volume printing or the tractor and combine for farming). However, some industries are confronted by both market and technological instability (for example, biotechnology, waste management), and the combination of these conditions cannot be adequately captured with an additive formula. Rather, the presence of technological volatility in a dynamic marketing context more than doubles the premium that a company would place on an innovative, risk-taking management team.

To help us grapple with the almost innumerable variety of interactions that can result from combinations of the four variables, Figure 5.3 suggests a quantitative approach to assessing the compensation-risk profile of a particular company. We devised a ten-point scale, from low to high risk, to account for each of the criteria discussed previously. To compute a composite risk profile, the ratings for all the factors are multiplied together and then divided by 100 to yield an overall rating that ranges from 0 to 100. The risk-profile classification at the bottom of this rating sheet provides a general guideline for categorizing any particular company. Note that the ranges for the classifications are not of equal width. This logarithmic specification of the ranges is necessary to accommodate the compounding effect of the factors and to adequately distinguish between higher- and lower-risk situations.

Figure 5.4 illustrates the practical application of these criteria for a wide range of companies in broadly differing industries. It is interesting to note that even companies in similar industries can have significantly

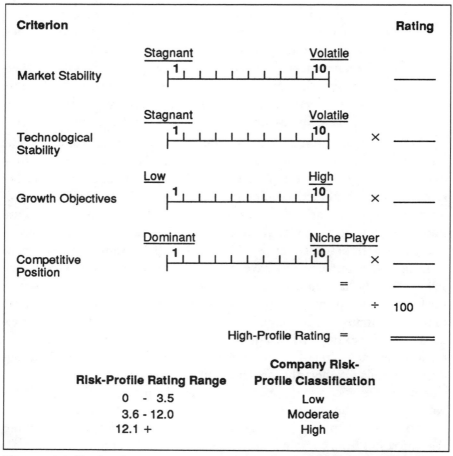

Figure 5.3 Evaluating a Company's Compensation-Risk Profile

different risk profiles. The well-established building-products manufacturer has one of the lowest-risk profiles, whereas the regional distributor of similar products to the same markets has a considerably higher-risk profile. Looking at two manufacturers in the office-furniture business, one a high-end design leader in the industry and the other a low-end price competitor, yields a similar contrast in risk profiles.

In the realm of compensation planning, a desperate search for the "unified field theory" that can explain all compensation phenomena is endemic to the discipline. So the policy planner should be aware that the thresholds defined for the risk-profile categories in Figure 5.4 should not be taken too literally. They are based solely on our experience with a

Factor Rating

Industry/Company	Market Stability	Technological Stability	Growth Objectives	Competitive Position	Composite Rating
Commercial finance	8	3	9	8	17.3
Building products manufacturing	4	2	3	2	0.5
Building products distribution	7	2	7	5	4.9
Consumer appliances	2	4	2	2	0.3
International banking software	3	8	8	7	13.4
Office furniture manufacturing (Company 1)	4	6	4	3	2.9
Office furniture manufacturing (Company 2)	4	4	7	6	6.7
Travel incentive administration	3	3	7	7	4.4
Industrial tissue products	1	5	2	3	0.3
Business direct marketing systems	3	5	6	7	6.3
Directory advertising publications	2	2	4	2	0.3
Textbook publishing	2	2	5	5	1.0
Jewelry manufacturing and retailing	4	3	6	6	4.3
Pharmaceutical manufacturing	5	8	6	6	14.4

Figure 5.4   Sample of Compensation-Risk Profile Evaluations

sample of perhaps 150 companies. Moreover, a paradox similar to the one applicable when measuring market share arises when the risk-profile categories are determined. The categories are to some extent dependent on how an organizational unit is configured, just as market share is dependent on how the market is delineated. If the scope of an organizational unit is defined too narrowly, the use of this profile classification may become arbitrary and can result in internal compensation inequity. On the other hand, defining the organizational unit too broadly (for example, attempting to apply the risk profile to a holding company made up of 20 separate operating companies) would also be meaningless. Thus, this tool of classification is useful only when the boundaries of market, technology, and competition are readily identifiable.

Now that a context for a company's risk policy has been established, the next step is to look at individual positions and create a method for assessing their risk profile. The inner core of the model (Figure 5.2) depicts five independent criteria that combine in the same compounding manner as the company factors to determine the risk profile of a given position. It is important to remember, however, that this evaluation, like its forerunner for the total company, provides only a relative scale of risk. For the company evaluation, the profile provided a basis of comparison across *different* companies; the individual position evaluation provides a scale for comparing the "riskiness" of positions *within* a company. As before, some clarification of these criteria is a necessary starting point:

■ **Scope of Influence.** Some positions in an organization influence a wide variety of activities, whereas others have a much more narrowly confined sphere of influence. As the sphere of influence narrows, it is usually easier to define and isolate performance, and for positions of this character, compensation risk is more readily accepted. In concrete terms, a salesperson's sphere of influence is quite narrow, that of a product or plant manager is somewhat broader, and that of a corporate controller or legal counsel is even wider. Ironically, because the sphere of influence of the CEO is all-encompassing, the results for this position can also be isolated easily. So the real challenge to the compensation planner is to be objective in his or her assessment of this factor for the majority of the positions that fall in the middle, where the scope of activity may be broad and the insularity of results can vary widely.

■ **Reaction Time.** Initiative is crucial when a position's environment necessitates quick response to immediate circumstances. If a plant personnel manager must confer with the corporate labor relations director every time a grievance arises, the credibility of the entire plant-management team is diminished. On the other hand, rarely will even a CEO be put in a position where a quick, situational decision must be rendered without the counsel of the top management team. Thus, short reaction time places a premium on individual initiative that can apply at middle- and lower-levels of an organization, and not necessarily at the top.

■ **Execution Proximity.** The degree of direct control a position exercises on the results for which it is held accountable is an important facet of the risk profile, but, contrary to conventional thought on this subject, it is not the dominant factor. This facet incorporates the concept of reporting level (which is just another name for the horizontal taxonomy assailed in an earlier discussion) but also extends to gauge a position's involvement in the front-line implementation of strategic or tactical initiatives. Contrasting this factor with "independence of action" (see below), a sales representative usually will have a high rating on execution proximity, but if policy constrains the representative's decision-making prerogatives (for example, in setting prices), then the position's independence of action rating would be relatively low. In this construct, even though a superficial analysis would suggest that the chief financial officer of a company is far removed from strategic or tactical execution, the direct involvement of this position in capital allocation decisions would grant it a high execution proximity score.

■ **Independence of Action.** Few would argue that the CEO of a company has anything less than the widest latitude for independent action of all the positions in an organization. But this obvious conclusion does not necessarily lead to corollary statements about each of the positions directly reporting to the CEO. Nor does it translate further down the organization into a gradually dissipating sense of independence. On the contrary, the research scientist in the laboratory and the supervisor on the plant floor should be encouraged to think independently and take initiative if their functions are crucial to the tactical or strategic success of a company.

Practically speaking, the overriding consideration for this factor is the management style of the CEO and the senior management team. If decision making is highly centralized, with policies and procedures confining most middle- and lower-level management prerogative, then any encouragement of individual initiative will produce only a disconcerting effect throughout the organization. If the converse is true, a higher tolerance for pay risk is more likely.

∎ **Consequence of Action.** This factor is perhaps the primary counterbalance to all the others, and it builds on the notion of one-way and two-way impact mentioned in chapter 1. Positions with a narrow scope of responsibility that require quick, situational responses and that are given a wide latitude for independent action will have a high-risk profile only if the consequences of their actions are significant. Similarly, a CEO whose scope of influence is quite broad, whose reaction time is self-paced, and so forth, takes actions only of high consequence. Thus, the risk profile for this position is also counterbalanced by the consequence factor. Risk should track with consequence. It makes little sense to spend a lot of time paying for easily measured results that are of modest consequence; and conversely, it is worthwhile to spend a lot of time searching for the right measures of performance, even if they are difficult or complex to define, if the consequences of action are high.

Another aspect of this factor is the manager's influence on strategic versus tactical decisions. Strategic decisions are naturally characterized by a higher degree of irrevocability, leading to far-reaching consequences for a company. Such decisions require vision, confidence, and a tolerance for the "peril of purpose" that can be constructively reinforced with at-risk pay policy.

Putting these five factors together in the same manner that the company profile was constructed yields a similarly convenient and quantitative method for appraising the compensation-risk profile of a position. In Figure 5.5, each of the factors is arrayed on a ten-point scale, and a composite rating is derived for the position. These ratings are then used as the basis for assigning a position to a risk category, illustrated in Figure 5.6. As a general guideline, the following table can be used to bracket compensation mix for the risk categories:

Risk Classification	Compensation Risk as a Percentage of Base Salary
Team builder	Less than 10%
Individual achiever	10%–25%
Principal contributor	25%–40%
Stakeholder	40%–75%
Entrepreneur	Over 75%

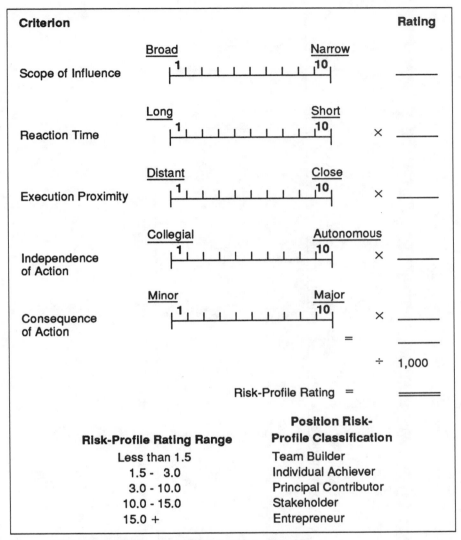

Figure 5.5 Evaluating a Position's Risk Profile

The final risk amounts for each position within each category are determined by superimposing the company risk profile on the prescribed position risk range. Companies with a high-risk profile tend to set individual position compensation risk at the high end of the range; the opposite occurs with low-risk companies.

As we couple this new compensation-mix concept with the performance-unit theme introduced in the previous chapter, the definition of an

Position	Scope of Influence	Reaction Time	Execution Proximity	Independence of Action	Consequence of Action	Composite Rating
CEO	10	2	8	10	10	16.0
Corporate controller	3	4	4	4	4	0.8
Top marketing and sales executive	6	5	7	6	8	10.1
Corporate development executive	6	2	7	3	8	2.0
Strategic planning executive	3	3	3	2	6	0.3
Brand manager	8	5	7	5	7	9.8
Plant manager	7	4	8	6	5	6.7
Sales representative	8	8	9	6	4	13.8
Engineering section manager	4	4	8	3	3	1.1

Figure 5.6 Sample of Position-Risk Profile Ratings

appropriate incentive structure for the firm should come more clearly into focus. And when the compensation planner uses the prescribed framework for integrating risk policy with organizational and job analysis, thoughtful design rather than happenstance will govern whether compensation is equitably and effectively used to reinforce organizational accountabilities, decision-making processes, and strategic priorities.

This chapter has demonstrated the intricacies of setting compensation-risk policy for a variety of positions whose characteristics differ greatly, up and down the organization and even within a salary grade or organizational reporting level. Together with a company's native compensation-risk propensity, the position-risk profile allows compensation policy to transcend survey data and achieve a custom fit to the organization. In the absence of this "third dimension" of job evaluation, true internal equity (that is, a concept of equity that fairly places a manager's compensation at risk dependent on his or her ability to affect contingent results) may remain an elusive target, and an opportunity to strengthen the achievement-pay system may be missed.

6

Performance Measurement

In Search of Added Value

Pollster Daniel Yankelovich coined a phrase—"the McNamara fallacy"—to describe the Vietnam-era Defense Secretary's artful illusion in quantifying the war. McNamara's approach was first to measure what could easily be measured. Then, that which could not be measured easily was given an arbitrary quantitative value. As the media became more proactive in investigating the war, McNamara's next tactic was to pronounce that all of those things that could not be measured easily were not very important. And finally, when the war's premise came under intense public scrutiny, that which could not be measured easily was declared nonexistent.

The quantification of management performance is unfortunately susceptible to this same fallacy. As corporations seek to quantify success, they can find many easily measured results that are superficially appealing; but, like McNamara's statistics, they are only half-truths that give clues to the full performance picture while artfully omitting the more arcane and insightful portrayals of management's "value added." The effect of the McNamara fallacy on incentive-plan design is predictable. For the past 20 or 30 years incentive plans have reflected an accountant's perspective, pandering to the lowest common denominator of the investing public by linking payouts to return on stockholders' equity, earnings per share, company pretax profits, and other bottom-line measures.

It is scarcely a new thought (only one that is summarily ignored in the compensation arena) that managers cannot manage the bottom line but must ride the frontier—between analysis and action, value and return, the present and the future—in the pursuit of financial success. At the top of a company, the trade-offs may be as straightforward and readily apparent as growth versus profitability (so long as it is clear which measures of growth and which measures of profitability best fit the business). But at each successive level below the CEO, the trade-offs proliferate, and the balancing act required to unify the organization's energy becomes more intricate. In short, if compensation planners continue to ignore this intricacy, the final two steps of McNamara's fallacy will catalyze the disintegration of achievement pay as a vital management tool.

The Many Faces of Simplicity

While supposedly seeking a broadly understood and easily communicated yardstick for calibrating a company's welfare or, more narrowly, the performance of a particular organizational unit, compensation-policy planners are seduced by the apparent simplicity of one-dimensional, generic measures like net earnings. In fact, these policymakers are often tempted to treat "simplicity" as the foremost criterion in guiding the design of their incentive programs. However, if design simplicity is placed at the hub of the compensation-policy wheel, the directional purposes of incentives can be lost in the wake of such a simpleminded focus, and the KISS principle, so easily invoked, may become a universal pretext for accepting this policy Pablum.

The simplicity criterion, though broadly applied, is amorphous. Its overuse, as well as management's interpretations of its reciprocal, complexity, has produced a vast array of alternative meanings. Thus, we begin this chapter with an urgent plea that, before the directional thrust of an incentive plan is sacrificed for the sake of simplicity, the compensation planner understand which of the following complaints management is expressing when it rejects a plan's design because of its inherent "complexity."

Administrative Work Load

Any performance measure must pass a validity test that compares the cost of tracking results with the value the company derives from closely managing the selected dimension of performance. No performance measure or tracking system should be created solely for the purpose of an incentive program. If the information on results is not otherwise important to the management of a performance unit, then it most certainly should not be tracked exclusively for the incentive program. But determining whether important performance objectives are actually achieved may require deeper analysis than is readily available in an income statement. If performance measures are directional to the extent that they reflect not only a result but also the trade-offs that are made en route to that result, then monitoring performance may require additional administrative record keeping, and installation of the incentive system will usually necessitate training rather than just communication.

Short-term versus long-term, profit versus growth, and return versus diversification are just some of the most obvious examples of the decision trade-offs that management is asked to make in the interests of the shareholders. And few managers would argue that the success of a business can be measured on a one-dimensional scale. Consequently, incentive performance measures and the operating mechanics of an incentive plan must attempt to encompass the critical decision-making nodes inherent in a company's strategy. However, in this attempt pure simplicity and a "straightforward" message may be sacrificed.

As an example of a plan that some companies might reject for its administrative complexity, consider one that was developed for the group executives of a medium-sized holding company. As in many companies of this type, at the beginning of each year the group executives are given a set of objectives for improving the results of the operating companies. In one company, the rationalization of manufacturing operations may be the dominant concern, whereas at another the integration of a new acquisition (systems, sales force, personnel policies) can be the principal focus. Even though these priorities are quite clear at the beginning of the year, past experience indicated that it was normal for other priorities to surface during the year as additions to the original objectives.

In designing the group executives' incentive program, then, we needed to accommodate these shifting priorities without severely diluting the original focus. The company adopted an incentive system in which the original priorities were incorporated into a composite performance profile that was in turn coupled to an incentive payout schedule. As priorities changed during the year, the CEO made brief notes to ensure that the new objectives were incorporated into the performance profile. When it came time to determine the final bonus payments, the augmented list of objectives was reweighted, and the payout scale was extended to provide a higher payout at target performance. (In chapter 8, the details of this incentive concept, along with many other structural variations, are discussed.) In this system, an important provision precludes maximum payout unless some change and expansion in the priorities occur during the year. Given this company's dynamic environment, part of senior management's implicit performance standard is adaptability, and this unconventional feature of the incentive program is designed to reward for the "flex" in the manager's responsibilities. But the tracking and administrative system required to accommodate this flex necessarily adds a degree of complexity, and this essential feature could be rejected for its administrative burden by a management less committed to achievement pay.

Objective-Setting Difficulties

To put it in simplest terms, the business planning process is founded on two sets of assumptions—business environment (economic and competitive conditions) and the expected results of strategy execution. This process is the same whether the business is the manufacture of chewing gum or automobiles, yo-yos or industrial chemicals; a chain of personal-computer stores; or the production of stainless steel. The market forces outside the control of management along with the organization's internal competencies exert the delimiting pressures that shape a company's strategy. With this strategy in hand, a company then projects annual and long-term business results (for example, profits, market share, sales growth) that embody confidence in a chosen direction and in the ability of the organization to follow that course. Ironically, at the same time this scenario is set, the business planners often willfully acknowledge the practical reality of several alternative scenarios.

The compensation planner's dilemma is that, while confronted with these inexorable uncertainties, he or she must devise some method for linking pay to performance objectives. Routinely, the "most-likely" scenario for the business is selected as the immutable basis for incentive payouts while other very real possibilities fade into oblivion. Though this solution passes most tests for simplicity, its single-mindedness and disregard of alternative scenarios drives a wedge between compensation policy and all other performance-management processes.

Another approach the compensation planners can take that is not quite so dependent on the accuracy of financial projections measures one company's performance against a peer group of companies in the same industry. For this approach to work, the planner must be confident that differences in the economy will affect all companies in the peer groups about equally. The trickiest decision in implementing this type of performance-measurement system however, is the identification of peer companies whose financial performance data are accessible and whose business mix is comparable to that of the planner's company.

Perhaps the most thoughtful solution to these objective-setting difficulties is to openly acknowledge the alternative business scenarios and to build two to four distinct performance profiles that reflect the varying conditions. For instance, executives of a large financial services company were dissatisfied with a bonus program that rewarded managers exclusively for performance relative to a preplanned profit objective. Recognizing that the company's financial welfare is heavily influenced by volatility in stock market transaction volume and average share price—conditions over which the company's executives have no control—any assessment of performance outside the context of these conditions is irrelevant. In fact, the true test of the managers' performance is how well they plan for and adapt to changing conditions rather than their accuracy in forecasting them.

To respond to these circumstances, we designed an incentive plan around an objective framework that specified three or four preset expectations for performance, depending on the market conditions (Figure 6.1). For each scenario, an acceptable performance range is defined as the foundation for incentive payouts. Because the payout schedule was matched to the performance range consistently for all scenarios, an indelible feature of this system was that executive pay, at any given point in a performance range, was unaffected by business conditions. So, what was once in all but official terms strictly a profit-sharing arrangement is now recast to mitigate the influence of market conditions and to reward managers for their decisiveness in the face of these conditions.

Obstructions in the Line of Sight

While searching for the single all-encompassing performance measure, a few thought leaders have engineered notable advances in incentive-

Average Share Price	Return-on-Equity Performance Range	
	Transaction Volume	
	High	Low
High	Scenario 1: 50%–70%	Scenario 2: 30%–50%
Low	Scenario 3: 40%–60%	Scenario 4: 15%–35%

Performance within Scenario Range	Bonus Payout Rate
Minimum acceptable	10% of target bonus
Meeting expectations	100% of target bonus
Outstanding	150% of target bonus

Figure 6.1 The Multi-Plan Objective Framework

compensation technology beyond the tried-and-true formulas such as earnings per share. These advances include the intrinsic market value, discounted cash flow, economic value added, and return on invested capital models. Unfortunately, many of the benefits of these developments are lost because of the zigzag line of sight between standard accounting formats and these "more complex" presentations of financial data. It is also a reality that these concepts die on the vine because of top management's lack of commitment to the difficult communication task that is required for the establishment of these concepts in the company's performance-management system.

At lower levels in the organization where functional rather than general-management accountabilities dominate, a different barrier encroaches on the line of sight. The perennial complaint of middle managers, whose compensation is tied to bottom-line business-unit performance, is that they have only limited influence or control over these results. Thus, from their perspective the line of sight to these performance measures is obscured by intervention, and sometimes competition, from other functions. To allay this concern, compensation planners can move toward incentives that pay exclusively for functional performance, but with this approach comes the potential for suboptimization that can be offset only with multiple counterbalancing performance measures. The specter of complexity once again rears its ugly head, and these same planners typically retreat to the higher ground of generic, easily communicated bottom-line numbers.

The purpose of any "more-complex" performance measure, whether for general or functional management, is to broaden the manager's angle of view. Because they highlight critical intersections in the decision-making process, measures such as return on investment or intrinsic market value impel general managers to understand and become intimately involved in the transactions that flow from the income statement to the balance sheet. Similarly, counterbalancing functional measures accentuate the critical interdependencies *within* a business unit, instilling a middle-management accountability that is both sharply focused on controllable results and acutely sensitized to the broader business mission.

None of the "innovations" enumerated here should be considered revelations. These concepts have been bantered about in the business and academic communities for many years. But thus far the case for simplicity has dominated in the compensation arena, whereas in the performance-management arena, these more complex techniques have gained general acceptance. Consequently, the chasms between pay policy and management practice grow ever wider.

The Tale of the Tape

In these times of obsession with quick fixes and pop business psychology, there is no dearth of alternatives for measuring the results of a company or a performance unit. Almost all of these alternatives are promoted as proxies for the shareholders' interests; but with the raging debate on this subject, it is obviously pointless to continue the search for the perfect measure. In place of this search, the compensation planner should accept, at face value, the intrinsic connection between the company's strategy and the shareholders' interests and then assess alternative performance measures purely on the basis of their support of that strategy. To lay the foundation for this assessment, the principal features of some of the most frequently used performance indicators (categorized as either financial or functional) are described as follows.

Financial Measures

Financial measures are by their nature the household vernacular of accounting formulations that give only an inkling of a company's competitive strategy. They communicate, in terms of end results, what *has been* accomplished, and they are usually a summary statement that consolidates a wide range of income and balance sheet transactions:

▮ **Earnings**. In almost all companies, some earnings dialect is used as a standard for communicating management success or failure. Many companies speak the language of *pretax* earnings to filter out the isolated effects of tax accounting and accelerated depreciation policies. Others center on pretax *operating* earnings to cleanse the performance standards of the impurities (primarily interest expense and sometimes corporate allocations) attributable to a firm's financial structure. Finally, companies may divide their after-tax earnings by the number of common shares outstanding, yielding the ubiquitous earnings-per-share measure and signaling management's vaguely patronizing acknowledgment of the shareholders' interests. No matter which line item a company chooses to demarcate its profits, this bottom-line performance indicator should be used in incentive plans only for positions that inherently influence each line item in the income statement. To use it otherwise is to move variable pay out of the incentive arena and into the milieu of profit sharing.

▮ **Gross Revenues**. One rarely comes across a financial news item that does not comment on earnings and sales in the same breath. Most frequently commentators compare the growth in earnings to the growth in sales to discern whether a firm's profitability is on track. But taken alone, revenue measures have two hidden facets that can disguise true performance.

First, they must be configured with a realistic sense of what best describes the value produced by a company. A manufacturer will correctly zero in on the conventional definition of sales that captures the net proceeds from all transactions with its customers, since the manufacturer's mission is to add value by transforming raw and semifinished material into a finished product. In contrast, distribution companies are in essence providing a service whose value is most accurately depicted by the difference between gross sales and the cost of goods sold. If a distributor were to concentrate on gross sales rather than gross margin dollars, a potentially distorted view of success could emerge that would ignore the primary concerns of this business—product mix and margin. Yet another contrasting example, professional-service firms, must look to the net value contributed by their personnel resources as the true top-line measure. Including passed-through expenses (for example, media space and time purchases in the advertising industry, hotel bookings and air fares in the corporate travel business, or out-of-pocket expenses in the consulting sector) inflates the revenue line but provides little useful information on the productivity of internal resources.

The second reality of revenues is that they are meaningful only in the context of the marketplace. Real sales success occurs only when a new market or customer is penetrated, market share is captured from a competitor (or successfully protected), or a favorable (higher-margin) product substitution is realized. Sales growth that merely ebbs and flows with the general economic tide is a potentially deceptive indicator of management performance. Thus, the "quality" of sales is an important dimension of gross revenue dollars if a sales measure is used to gauge advances in a company's competitive performance.

■ **Growth.** In any of its manifestations, growth is seen as an indicator of financial health. Though business history is replete with examples of deleterious growth, its absence is almost universally regarded as a weakness.

Three distinct categories of growth capture different aspects of a company's activity. Income-statement growth is usually measured by top-line sales or bottom-line profits (or earnings per share). An incentive plan tied to this category of growth differs from those tied to absolute bench marks of sales or profits in that growth thresholds mandate a progression (even if it is nonspecific in its source). To see this contrast in action, look at the formula by which executive bonuses are funded at Boeing Company or at Ashland Oil. In both of these companies, 6 percent of after-tax income from the first dollar is contributed to a bonus pool. A growth-oriented formula, on the other hand, might specify that a company must achieve a certain percentage growth in earnings, say 10 percent, before the pool is funded at the 6 percent level; smaller contributions could be made for slower growth, and larger amounts for more rapid growth.

The second category of growth focuses on the equity or invested-capital attributes of the balance sheet. Though equity growth has the patina of a shareholder perspective, it can also be misleading in that manipulation of a firm's financial structure can readily swell the equity account without any real increase in shareholder value. Responding to this deficiency, some companies rely on invested-capital growth as a measure of developmental achievement. But for this measure to truly reflect growth in shareholder value, it must be coupled with a return measure that validates internal reinvestment decisions.

The vortex of today's incentive-compensation thought is embodied in the final category of growth-related measures. In this category, an attempt is made to capture the "true" growth in a company's market value. Some companies choose the direct method and rely solely on their company's stock price. Others, recognizing the vagaries of the financial markets, use analytical concepts that compare actual returns to the firm's cost of capital and assume that any surplus in this formula is an increment to shareholder value.

▌ **Returns.** Any financial-return ratio has a distinct advantage over the foregoing unitary measures, since ratios naturally counterbalance two divergent traits of an enterprise. The clear message of any incentive tied to a financial-return ratio is that managers must fix their eyes equally on the numerator and the denominator. To maximize return on sales, management's strategy is clearly directed to margin enhancement (product mix and pricing); and, as will be true for all return formulas, any emphasis on growth will probably require a separately planned objective. Returns whose denominator is in the balance sheet (either equity or invested capital) convey a slightly more complex message than income-statement returns. These measures should raise three questions simultaneously: Has the earnings objective been achieved? Have the earnings been reinvested or paid out as dividends? Have retained earnings been reinvested wisely? Although return on equity has an established legacy of board and shareholder appeal, its vulnerability to manipulation (for example, a company trading debt for equity or borrowing to pay dividends) should discourage its doctrinaire acceptance. On the other hand, invested capital returns direct management attention simultaneously to the line accounts of working capital, to the timing of fixed asset enhancements, and to the management of the income statement. With balance-sheet returns, as with their income-statement counterparts, it is often desirable to couple independent measures of growth in the components of the denominator with the return measure to mitigate the tendency toward stagnation in deference to higher returns.

Functional Measures

These measures usually convey clear instructions on how management expects a result to be accomplished and can thus be tailored to fit the narrow scope of influence and accountability of individual positions. The abundance of these measures is constrained only by the common sense of managers and the costs of tracking results. Therefore, to succinctly illustrate the application of functional measures, we have selected only a few familiar ones for discussion in this section. In all cases, the narrative concentrates on the central tensions between quality, cost, and volume that drive each function's behavior (Figure 6.2) and that mandate the use of counterbalancing incentive performance measures for functional units.

Marketing

The polestar of the marketing function is sales volume and market penetration. However, increased volume does not come cost-free. Distribution and selling costs eat away at margins but at the same time can enrich the customer's perception of service and personal attention. Tugging at the other end of the rope, the management of customer, product or service mix aims toward increasing the quality of sales (or the profitability of the business) by controlling margins.

Examples

Volume	Cost	Quality
Sales	Distribution consolidation	Product/service mix
Market share	Selling	Account profitability
Product development		Brand/location profitability
Average order size		

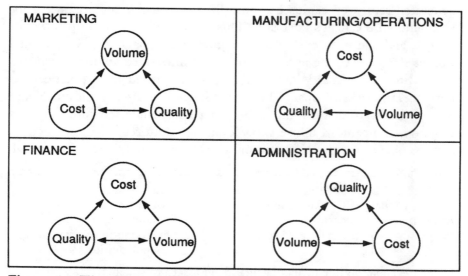

Figure 6.2 The Central Tensions of Functional Accountability

Manufacturing/Operations

None of the marketing function's profitability objectives can be accomplished without manufacturing's avidity in controlling costs. With cost at the apex of the accountability model, the manufacturing or operations manager helps bring into balance marketing's primary emphasis on volume. But a single-minded dedication to cost control or productivity improvement can create processing bottlenecks or severely impair the quality of the output. So the compensation planner cannot be satisfied with any general plant (or location) profitability measure for this function that does not pinpoint specific capital-productivity, technology-enhancement, and quality-assurance priorities.

Examples

Cost	Quality	Volume
Labor productivity	Fill rates	Manufacturing-cycle time
Scrap reduction	Reject rates	Technology upgrade
Inventory levels	Customer satisfaction	Physical output
Technology upgrade	Complaint volume	
	Technology upgrade	

Finance

Business success inevitably leads to cash generation that exceeds the appetite of a company for reinvesting funds. Therefore, in striving for an equilibrium between financial resource supply and demand, financial management's principal aim is to minimize the cost of capital through capital-structure and risk-management initiatives and to increase the internally generated return on capital by controlling the quality and volume of investments in the firm's portfolio. This mission is closely akin to that of a bank, and one need only recall the government bailout of Continental Illinois Bank to see the potential impact of unfettered volume incentives in the financial arena. Whether foreseen or learned from practical experience, the risks of financial function incentives are significant. Nonetheless, by crafting carefully stabilized performance measures for this function, companies can use variable pay to reinforce critical objectives and to enhance the margin between the return on and the cost of capital.

Examples

Cost	Quality	Volume
Cost of capital	Working capital turnover	Cash throwoff
Bad debts	Earnings "quality"	Economic value growth*
		Qualifying new investment opportunities

*Added economic value of incremental fixed-asset investments

— 130 —

Administration

The technical depth of resources, and the response time, reliability, accuracy and scope of services provided all contribute to the perception of added value and quality for administrative service functions. Once a commitment is made to provide a particular service, the quality standards that are established will dictate the cost of that service and the function's capacity for throughput. So neither volume nor cost can be arbitrarily adjusted without the company first assessing the impact on quality.

Examples

Quality	Cost	Volume
Transaction reliability	Organization development	Staff utilization
Project bench marks	Complaint levels	Vendor management
	Error rates	Project-budget variance
		Overhead-expense reduction

Sizing Up the Performance Measures

Two corporate executives met in the officers' dining room for lunch one day. "What's this I hear about you?" demanded one. "You say you don't believe in our company's pay-for-performance program?"

The reply was instant and indignant: "That's a lie. I never said I didn't believe in the pay-for-performance program. I *do* believe in it. It's the backbone of our management system. I would stake my career on the tenets of pay for performance. All I said was that I don't know what it means!"

When it comes to assessing the meaning of performance in terms that have personal financial value, today's managers are much like this indignant executive: They are quite willing to state their undying support of performance-based pay systems, but they do not really know, or accept, a definition of performance that sets personal-achievement expectations. This ambivalence is understandable in light of the many faces of performance that occur inside today's complex business organizations.

One of the recurring themes of this book is the inextricable linkage between strategy execution and performance-based pay. Up to this point, a solid foundation of compensation hierarchies, performance units, and pay risk has been constructed to support this linkage, but these concepts have not yet been directly associated with the tiers of strategic accountability and performance measurement in a business. Accordingly, the final stages of designing an achievement-pay system may be the most challenging, because the policy planner must clearly understand all facets of the strategy in order to justify each program feature.

According to the Hofer and Schendel monograph *Strategy Formulation: Analytical Concepts*, there are three major levels of organizational strategy: corporate, business unit, and functional area. The levels of strategy are further dissected into four components that are common to each level:

▌ **Scope.** A business is created by its domain, or the range of its products and market segments; the geography it serves; the technology it employs; or the distribution channels it uses. Whereas products and markets are the most conventional delimiters for a manufacturing business, technology, distribution, or geography may be more important in defining the scope for other types of businesses.

▌ **Resource Deployment.** No actions or goal achievements can take place at any level unless the company develops some basic skills by obtaining and deploying resources in a way that cannot be duplicated. Sometimes this process is referred to as the creation of distinctive competencies, and for the compensation planner, these distinctions should be of utmost concern in the design of performance measures for performance units, work teams, or individuals.

▌ **Competitive Advantage.** The position an organization develops vis-à-vis its competitors is the result of astute scoping of products and markets at the senior management level, and farther down the organization this market position is the result of applying the organization's skills in a manner that creates unique value for the market. Competitive advantage defines for the compensation planner the key business priorities that the performance measures should gauge.

▌ **Synergy.** Resource deployment and scoping decisions can work in concert, or they can work to negate each other. Synergy, from the compensation planner's perspective, is the goal of nurturing cooperation among disparate organizational units, thereby creating competitive advantage.

As Hofer and Schendel pointed out, strategy inherently has different connotations, and therefore different indicators of execution success, at each of its three levels. At the corporate level, the primary question is one of portfolio management—determining and adjusting the desired mix of businesses or product lines. The scope of the business and the way in which its primary resources—capital, information, personnel—are allocated and deployed is management's critical concern. The other strategic components—distinctive competencies and business-unit interaction—are of somewhat less importance at the corporate level, unless the interaction of selected units is a crucial contributor to competitive advantage. So at this level, performance measures should focus on management's degree of success in making adjustments to the portfolio and on the portfolio's overall financial return.

At the business-unit level, management's scope is narrowed, and its primary concern is competitive success in a particular industry or product/market segment. Thus, distinctive competencies—lowest cost, channel power, product innovation, and so on—that produce a competitive advantage are the primary concerns of management. The business-unit manager is also concerned with the scope of the business, but at this level, the focus is on managing the product life cycle and making choices about product/market segments. Also, the integration of functional areas in the organization to create a unified sense of purpose is a crucial influence of business-unit management. At this level, then, performance measures must penetrate beyond conventional financial ratios and zero in on the business unit's key success factors—introduction of new products, quality-assurance ratings, cash flows, and working-capital utilization.

The functional area is the third level of organization strategy and is primarily concerned with resource productivity. Thus, the indicators of performance tend to center on cost management, project-completion schedules, and the efficient flow of routine work. Through aggressive and creative execution of functional-level strategies, a company seeks unique ways to deploy its resources to ultimately provide a competitive advantage.

Performance-Measure Evaluation: Corporate

After the string of performance measures that we discussed in the glossary has been reviewed, a frame of reference for fitting these measures to the performance units is the next building block of compensation policy. Criteria expressly aligned with the company's business strategy and objectives should be used to compare and evaluate alternative measures. A prototype evaluation model developed for the senior executive group of a medium-sized (publicly held) manufacturing holding company is illustrated in Figure 6.3.

Evaluation Criteria/Weighting

Measures	Short-Term Stockholder Return (weight = 1)	Long-Term Stockholder Value (weight = 3)	Independence from Capital Structure (weight = 2)	Compatibility with unit RONA Measure (weight = 3)	Business-Portfolio Enhancement (weight = 2)	Peer-Group Comparability (weight = 1)	Ease of Communication (weight = 1)	Overall Rating
Earnings:								
NOPAT	◐	○	●	●	○	○	◐	◐
EPS	●	○	○	○	○	●	●	○ +
Pretax	◐	○	○	○	○	◐	●	○ +
Growth:								
Sales	○	○	●	◐	◐	●	●	◐
EPS	◐	◐	○	○	○	●	●	◐
Equity	◐	◐	○	○	○	○	○	○ +
Capital	◐	◐	●	◐	◐	◐	○	◐

Return:								
ROS	○	○	●	○	◑	○	●	◑
ROI	◑	◑	●	●	◑	●	◑	◑+
ROE	◑	◑	○	○	○	◑	●	○+
Growth/return combinations:								
Sales	○	○	●	○	◑	◑	◑	○+
Invested capital	◑	●	●	●	◑	●	◑	●
Equity	◑	◑	○	○	○	◑	○	○
EVA	◑	●	●	○	●	○	○	◑

Responsiveness to Criterion	
Above average	●
Average	◑
Below average	○

Figure 6.3 Corporate-Performance-Measure Evaluation Model

In the left-hand column of this model, 14 different performance measures are categorized and then evaluated relative to the criteria listed across the top of the table. Each of the evaluation criteria is assigned a weight (1, 2, or 3) based on the importance of the criterion to the company. The far-right-hand column tabulates the weighted averages of the ratings for each measure. According to this evaluation the combination of invested capital growth and return is the best choice for the holding company's senior-management financial-performance incentives. On the other hand, several measures, including earnings per share, return on equity, and a combination of growth and return on equity, are ill-matched to this company's priorities.

Though this may seem a tedious process by which a planner arrives at an intuitive conclusion, the discipline of clearly defining and weighting criteria to select performance measures frees the planner from the strict earnings-per-share mind-set and provides a forum for unthreateningly questioning a company's performance-management biases. Through this process, a wider range of alternatives is considered, and the debate on performance measures is rescued from the morass of preconceived conclusions and raised to the higher plane of strategic fit.

Let us look more closely at the evaluation to better understand the outcomes. The operating units of the holding company are all in mature, cyclical businesses servicing the transportation and industrial-equipment markets. Some of these companies enjoy a dominant position in their markets, whereas others are being restructured to enter new markets or to solidify their current market position. As a growing and successful holding company, it is constantly reevaluating its portfolio, but acquisitions and divestitures are regularly diverting the operating-unit focus of the senior-management team. In this environment, the performance-measure evaluation criteria and their respective weightings reflect the following mix of board-member biases and strategy imperatives:

▮ **Short-Term Stockholder Return.** With publicly traded stock, the company found it impossible to avert the investment community's scrutiny of quarterly earnings reports. To exclude any reference to short-term profits in measuring performance would be self-defeating, but, recognizing the longer-term perspective needed to manage virtually all of the operating units, management was reluctant to align itself completely with the board viewpoint by heavily weighting this criterion.

▪ **Long-Term Stockholder Value.** If the cyclical demand of these mature businesses were allowed to rule the decision-making processes, management would be tempted to turn its back on the next phase of the cycle (up or down) in favor of the current phase. And because the operating units would be ill-prepared to gain competitive ground in the next cycle, their economic future would be in jeopardy. Thus, all levels of management strongly concurred that this criterion should be heavily weighted.

▪ **Independence from the Capital Structure.** Management believed that changes in the capital structure of the holding company had little or no impact on its long- or short-term performance. Moreover, any changes made in the structure were initiated by the executive committee of the board. Thus, for any financial performance criterion to have incentive value, it must be insulated from these restructuring decisions.

▪ **Compatibility with Operating-Company Performance Measures.** This company had worked diligently for more than five years to create a palpable connection between business planning and incentive compensation, and it understood all too well the fraility of this bond. Any hint that the corporate and operating-company goals were at cross-purposes would quickly diminish the credibility of the incentive program and its influence on strategy execution.

▪ **Business-Portfolio Enhancement.** In a holding company environment, the mission of the corporate executive team, simply stated, is to manage the portfolio of investments. To carry out this mission, management must first ensure, through its internal capital-appropriation decisions, that any reinvestment of assets enhances the portfolio's return. Second, in looking at any quantum additions or deletions to the portfolio, it is crucial that management keep the risk/return relationships in proper balance. As indicated in the evaluation model, only one measure, economic value added, comprehensively considers both sides of this equation. But even this measure, with its reliance on the problematic and somewhat subjective cost of capital determination, poses substantial communication barriers if used for incentive-compensation purposes.

▪ **Peer-Group Comparability.** In communicating with the board of directors, the CEO was constantly searching for touchstones to help explain the fortunes and misfortunes of the operating companies. Since most of the board members possessed only general knowledge of the businesses, a comparison to similar companies in an industry segment was a useful tool to enhance their understanding of performance. Management's weighting of this criterion therefore reflects a compromise between what measures were needed to manage the business and what were needed for board relations.

■ **Ease of Communication.** With its experience in building an intimate relationship between performance management and compensation, this company had learned that communication barriers are not insurmountable if management has a genuine commitment to the principles of a program. At the same time, it recognized that the introduction of foreign-sounding performance concepts can be disruptive in the short-term while a new decision-making vocabulary is evolving. It acknowledged this concern with the inclusion of a communication criterion.

To illustrate the application of the model using these seven criteria, a recap of the evaluation for the invested-capital growth/return combination measure is useful. Return on invested capital, as it stands alone without the capital-growth component, is a reasonably good measure of short-term stockholder return, but it fails to communicate the sharp earnings and shareholder focus of current-year earnings per share. Coupled with a capital-growth target, though, this combination provides an excellent correlation with stockholder value, because it forces simultaneous consideration of current returns and long-term reinvestment in the capital base.

Let us take the remaining criteria one at a time. If it is assumed that NOPAT (net operating profits after tax) is used as the numerator of the ROI calculation, then the independence of the performance measures from the capital structure is complete. Also, since the RONA (return on net assets) measure used in each operating company's incentive program is a direct analogue of ROI at the corporate level, these measures are highly compatible. This combination of measures also fares well with the portfolio-enhancement criterion, since its long-term capital-growth aspect forces a continuing assessment of the risk and returns of the portfolio business mix.

Although earnings per share is readily accessible in the financial reports of most peer companies, the comparison of either aspect of this combination measure can be equally accessible with a little number-crunching. Finally, ease of communication is a relative concern. Because the company had several years of experience working with RONA at its operating companies, coupling growth to this measure was not a major stumbling block. In fact, it was seen as a necessary adjunct to the well-established capital-budgeting process.

Now that we have stepped rather methodically through this litany of performance measures and evaluation criteria, it is important to remember that the compensation planner should use this model only as a prototype, since the performance measures are not all-inclusive and the evaluation criteria were selected to fit the needs of this particular holding company. In like manner, as this narrative moves on to the remaining strategy levels— business unit and functional area—only skeletal outlines of the analytical process, rather than the virtually boundless array of possible criteria and measures, are provided to catalyze the planner's thinking.

Performance-Measure Evaluation: Business Unit

The definition of a business unit may not always be as readily apparent as in the previous example of the holding company with its independent operating units. As a general guideline, for an organizational segment to qualify as a business unit, accountability for costs *and* revenues must be a bona fide dimension of management responsibility. However, in applying this template, the policy planner should be sensitive to the source of revenues and certain costs. If substantial accounting allocations rather than directly attributable revenues and costs comprise the income statement, it may be more appropriate to reclassify the business unit as a functional area and to measure performance on the basis of controllable expenses. Legitimate balance-sheet accountability, if it is comprehensive, can also be an acid test for distinguishing between business units and functional areas and determining the resources under a manager's control. Recalling the focal point of business-unit strategy—distinctive competence through functional integration—the business-unit analytical model shown in Figure 6.4 can be used as a springboard for custom-tailoring the evaluation criteria to any company's unique circumstances.

As at the corporate level, the business unit's strategy should be clearly evident in the weighting of the evaluation criteria. If, for example, the unit is in a mature industry and has an established and stable market position, cash throw-off may be management's primary objective, and the capital-utilization and functional-priority-balancing criteria would be given the heaviest weighting. If, conversely, the unit is in an aggressive building mode, the emphasis will probably be placed on competitive po-

Evaluation Criteria/Weights

Measures	Capital Utilization (weight =)	Functional Priority Balancing (weight =)	Competitive-Positioning Advancement (weight =)	Product/Market Portfolio Enhancement (weight =)	Compatibility with Corporate Measures (weight =)	Ease of Communication (weight =)	Overall Rating
Financial:							
Pretax earnings							
Return on sales							
Capital turnover							
RONA							
Sales growth							
Earnings growth							
Invested capital return/growth							
New-product sales							
Product-line profitability							
Market segment/ customer profitability							
Market share							
Organization realignment							

Responsiveness to Criterion	
Above average	●
Average	◐
Below average	○

Figure 6.4 Business-Unit Performance-Measure Evaluation Model

sitioning and portfolio enhancement. Finally, the criteria for corporate compatibility and ease of communication are necessary checkpoints to ensure that the measures selected bear the test of reason and do not outpace the performance-management system.

The performance measures in the left-hand column differ from the corporate measures by the addition of the strategy-execution milestones. This list, though clearly not exhaustive, is representative of the wide range of initiatives that cannot be adequately gauged or managed with pure financial measures but can be crucial to the fulfillment of a business unit's mission.

Performance-Measure Evaluation: Functional Area

Perhaps the most challenging hurdle to overcome in introducing functional-area incentives is suboptimization. Measures at this level in an organization bear a much higher risk of being literally interpreted by incentive participants and of causing precipitate changes in their behavior. Consequently, these measures must be precisely defined and scoped in terms that guard against one function gaining at the expense of another function (see Figure 6.5).

A story told by the president of a plumbing-supply distribution company illustrates the power (and peril) of functional incentives. The truck drivers for this company received incentive pay for meeting delivery schedules. One day a driver was delivering material to a new company warehouse and was given specific instructions to avoid a low railroad overpass by following a circuitous back-road route to the facility. With map in hand, the driver took the longer route and arrived slightly behind schedule at the warehouse. About 30 minutes later, after the truck was unloaded and had left the dock for its next stop, the president received a phone call and was told that one of the company's trucks was wedged in an overpass. It seems that the scope of the driver's instructions failed to specify the return route. Obviously, the hidden trade-off in this incentive program for on-time delivery was the potential it posed for careless driving.

But even after the compensation planner has satisfied the scope criteria and has identified the hidden trade-offs in the measures, he or she must be convinced that any proposed performance standard can be reliably tracked at a cost that is not disproportionate to the anticipated benefit. Irrespective of their popularity, functionally based gain-sharing programs, such as the Scanlon plan, can also cause management to lose its perspective

Measures	Evaluation Criteria/Weighting				Overall Rating
	Scope (weight =)	Measurability (weight =)	Administrative Cost/Complexity (weight =)	Compatibility with Business Unit Measures (weight =)	
Labor productivity					
Cost reduction					
Project completion					
Complaint volume					
Rejection quotas					
Safety/lost man-hours					
Service response time					

Responsiveness to Criterion

Above average	●
Average	◐
Below average	○

Figure 6.5 Functional-Area Performance-Measure Evaluation Model

on this cost/benefit balance. One prominent user of the Scanlon program cited a typical example of form triumphing over substance in the company's human resources department. In management's zeal to fulfill this gain-sharing program's requirement for a quantifiable performance measure, a variant on the McNamara fallacy emerged. With the selection of "open personnel requisition days" as the department's measure, neither the quality nor the cost-control mission of this administrative function (see Figure 6.2) was served. Rather, a quantifiable but irrelevant volume measure of one of the department's less important accountabilities was to be tracked with a time-consuming new record-keeping system.

To avoid these pitfalls, compensation planners will sometimes use company-wide cost measures supplemented by a participative management program or suggestion system. In these cases (the Improshare system is a good example), the administrative complexity is reduced, but the incentive impact of the program is diluted by obstructions in the employees' line of sight to these more generic performance measures. In summary, the watchwords for the compensation planner installing incentives at a functional-area level are exactness and common sense.

The Jagged Line to Strategic Performance

The leading edge of present-day compensation practice leads one step beyond the standard financial measures evaluated in the last section and reaches into the realm of competitive strategy. This strategic-compensation school relies heavily on the premise that financial performance incentives alone lack the scope to encourage managers to make an honest assessment of the long- and short-term performance trade-offs. Furthermore, members of this school argue that incentive elements should be tied to interim milestones of achievement along the path to longer-term results.

Though these arguments have obvious merit, adopting a strategic-compensation philosophy forces management to commit to a series of steps in the implementation of a strategy rather than solely to its end result. Companies often view this commitment to strategic execution as a roadblock to using strategic elements in an incentive program, since many managers as well as board compensation-committee members feel that any objective "above the bottom line" is redundant or lacks real substance. Perhaps the best example of this myopia is the often-expressed resistance companies have toward incentive payments for modifying the business mix (that is, customer or product-line concentration) even when this initiative is a key element of strategy for a company.

A formula for overcoming this management skepticism and for selecting substantive strategic milestones can be found in an evaluation grid for grading alternative programmatic objectives. The grid (Figure 6.6) groups objectives into three categories: strategic revenues (or market share), operations improvements, and value engineering of the product portfolio. Note that the focus of the objectives shifts dramatically from one hypothetical business unit to another as the mission of each unit dictates varying growth and return priorities, and these objectives rise above the influence of short-term economic or competitive shocks.

Alone, this evaluation grid may still fall short in convincing management that programmatic goals are not part of normal responsibilities and only create the facade of objectivity for an otherwise purely discretionary bonus plan. To help management overcome this objection and to ensure that the goals do not promote a deceptive image, strategic milestones should next be subjected to a three-step qualification test:

- **Personal Time Commitment.** The milestone demands a significant personal time commitment by the manager that cannot be diluted by delegation to internal or external resources.
- **Strategic Impact.** A substantive impact on the company's long-term performance is intrinsic to the milestone.
- **Resource Diversion.** A diversion of existing resources from normal activities is required to bring about the milestone's accomplishment.

Added Value: A Road Less Traveled

To paraphrase Bruce D. Henderson, founder of the Boston Consulting Group, GAAP accounting results, though useful as points of comparison, can be insidiously misleading as measures of management's added value. In Henderson's view, the real value of any business is one thing only: the cash it will return to its shareholders and the timing of these payments. Strategy must therefore look beyond GAAP to the trade-offs between the present and the future and between the interim accounting symbols and the reality.

Henderson points out the following in a 1977 essay:

Objective Type	Prospective Spin-off	Cash Generator	High Growth	Turnaround
Strategic revenue	Protect key customer revenue	Improve customer mix or customer profitability Selective targeting of new customers	Aggressive share acquisition	Market diversification Customer-base rationalization
Operations improvement	Rationalize inventories Streamline organization	Selective enhancement of production capacity	Capacity expansion Technology investment Organization development Systems development Vertical integration	Rebuild organization Establish management systems Consolidate production
Value added	Increase margin mix of sales	Enhancement of product "bundle"	New product introductions	Product extensions Product elimination

Figure 6.6 Classification of Corporate or Business-Unit Strategic Objectives

The difference between reported accounting profit and actual future value often presents extraordinary opportunities for a strategy to use the logic of a competitor as a weapon against him. For example, management bonuses for this year based (exclusively) on this year's return on assets are a symbol of a competitor's blindness and strategy illiteracy. Most current returns on assets are only checkpoints on the results of resource allocations made long ago and payoffs sometime far in the future. The checkpoints on a successful strategy plan are rarely on a straight line course.

Perhaps by the next century business leaders will take note of Henderson's views and will design performance measures that transform incentive systems into viable strategic weapons. But to bring about this performance-pay perestroika, top management and board compensation committees must first share strong convictions that compensation can in fact be used to influence and direct management behavior. Surprisingly, this conviction cannot be assumed. Furthermore, there must be a commitment up and down the organization to encourage challenge and debate of company strategy and performance assumptions, and to reject the mimickry that pervades incentive-plan design practices.

7

Cats, Dogs, Cows, and Compensation

Step by step, this book has been drawing incentive policy and business strategy closer together. We started the process by laying a policy foundation grounded in a total-compensation hierarchy, breaking away from traditional base-salary structures that stratify the organization and impede the matching of risk compensation to individual position accountabilities. Freed from the confines of a base-salary structure, performance units were then organized around distinct business missions, and the mix between fixed and at-risk pay was related to a position's decision-making authorities and the desired level of individual initiative. In chapter 6, the bond between incentive policy and strategy was further reinforced with the introduction of an analytical process for matching performance measures with various levels of strategy.

In this chapter, the final steps required to solidify this bond focus on two salients of incentive design—payable performance range and the mix of financial- and strategic-milestone performance measures. For this analysis, business strategy is classified based on the competitive conditions surrounding a business as well as a company's posture and response to these conditions. These classifications have evolved through many stages, first as an outgrowth of the product life cycle, and more recently as the now (in)famous business-portfolio-management concept.

Notwithstanding their popularity, these industry-growth and market share prescriptions have failed to take a foothold in the compensation arena. And up to this point, the compensation-design variables discussed in this book have related exclusively to an individual position's characteristics—accountabilities, authorities, and strategic impact, or a performance unit's strategy level—corporate, business-unit, or functional-area. But, like changes to individual accountabilities, major shifts in a business's approach to its market must also be reflected in the message delivered by the compensation program; consequently, it is equally important that compensation policy match the type of business in which a manager works.

As we have stated previously, compensation planning has not historically stood out in relief as a valued contributor when advances like the portfolio concept are made in business management and analysis. Winston Churchill once assessed his inspirational role in World War II in terms that ring true for the compensation planner: "It was the nation and the race dwelling around the globe that had the lion's heart. I had the luck to be called upon to give the roar. I also hope I sometimes suggested to the lion the right place to use his claws." To be sure, compensation planners have heartily endorsed the connections between pay and strategy execution, but when all the dust has settled, the planner's claws have remained sheathed, and timeworn (and too-familiar) design principles have almost always prevailed. As we add this one last dimension to the strategy connection, the growth/share logic that strategically separates dogs, cats, and cash cows should give the planner a literal template for applying the claws of compensation structure in the right places to achieve the desired fit with a wide variety of management missions in different types of businesses. In this way, the mix and weighting of performance measures and the thresholds of the payable performance range—performance levels below and above which incremental incentives are *not* paid—are matched to the growth/share strategies so that the resulting incentive package blends both positional and performance-unit traits.

Business-Strategy Paradigms

In the early 1970s, several models for business-strategy formulation became popular as "cookbooks" to guide analysis of a product line's or a business unit's competitive position. Each of these recipes suggests specific management imperatives and strategies aligned with the competitive classification of the business. Though the intervening years have dulled the sheen of these management models and enthusiasm for strategic planning has waned, the models can still provide an insightful analytical tool for setting compensation policy. But before we explore how these models can be used to design incentive programs, it is worthwhile to review the basic concepts of two of the more prominent paradigms.

Product Life Cycle

A product's growth or an industry's evolution is, according to the life-cycle model, analogous to the biological phases of birth, growth, and death. As many as eight stages, which follow an S-shaped revenue curve, have been used to describe this cycle of an industry's products. Recent popular literature offers a consolidated, four-stage view of the cycle (see Figure 7.1). Note that although early research on the cycle focused exclusively on individual manufactured products, subsequent theory has been extended to cover complete industry segments as well as the service

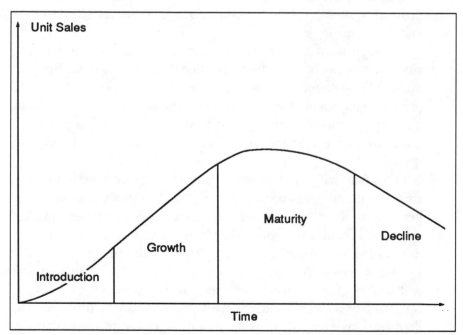

Figure 7.1 Product-Sales Life Cycle

sector. So the reader should interpret the following descriptions as applying equally to services, products, and industries.

▮ **Product Introduction.** During a product's debut in the marketplace, mutual experimentation by the producer and the consumer takes place. Ultimately, they reach a consensus on the product's market value. During this stage of experimentation and "settling in," profit is not the producer's primary objective; instead, market visibility and share development are the key indicators of commercial viability and are management's principal focal points. Certainly, return on investment is never too distant from anyone's mind during this stage; consequently, management must always be alert for market signals that invalidate the assumptions underlying the investment strategy or that threaten future profitability.

▮ **Market Growth.** In the growth stage, rapidly increasing profitability substantiates a product's commercial viability, but its growing market visibility also attracts potential competitors. With increased competitive pressure and the emergence of product variations and refinements, the producer is now faced with the challenge of protecting the investment. The cornerstone of this defense is a well-planned, well-executed value-engineering and product-technology-enhancement program.

Although management may be confident during the growth period, this is not a time for relaxation. Margins and profits will eventually peak and then begin to decline as a result of growing price pressures and market saturation. Management's most difficult challenge at this stage is to remain objective in assessing the potential of the business and to be attentive to signs of its encroaching maturity.

▮ **Market Maturity.** This stage is characterized by a period of entrenchment. As sales continue to rise and profits diminish, competitors reach an equilibrium that defines their permanent market position. Pressure to reduce operating costs forces product standardization and places greater emphasis on the intangible dimensions of competition, such as customer service (for manufacturers) and quality (for service businesses). In the previous two stages, operating costs were squeezed while the integrity of product standards was maintained, but as the product ages and reaches maturity, the standards themselves are scrutinized as management considers making changes in the product that yield additional cost efficiencies or that segregate the high and low price segments of the market.

- **Sales Decline.** Entry into this fourth and final stage of the life cycle also brings significant change to management's mission. Now the priority is to drain the last ounce of profit from the business and to minimize further investment. As in the introductory stage, management's acuity in reading the market signals is indispensable in judging when to pull the plug on the enterprise.

Though helpful, the life-cycle model is not conclusive, even in a macro sense, when it comes to the formulation of compensation policy. It provides useful insight into how performance should be measured in each of the stages, but it fails to incorporate an individual company's competitive position as an equally significant influence on the compensation program. So, to create an all-encompassing macro model of compensation policy, a method for simultaneously viewing the industry characteristics and the company's competitive position is needed. Enter the growth/share grid.

Growth/Share Matrix

The creation of the now-familiar growth/share classification system for analyzing the competitive standing of a business is generally attributed to the Boston Consulting Group, but McKinsey & Co., General Electric, and Shell have contributed significant augmentations to the original concept. With this portfolio-analysis technique, a business is evaluated from two perspectives: the growth outlook for its industry (as in the product life-cycle model), and the company's relative share of the market. A business-unit classification scheme for positioning senior-management accountabilities in the growth/share matrix is shown in Figure 7.2, and the characteristics of each business type are briefly discussed as follows:

- **Lion.** (High growth, high relative share) More commonly referred to as a *star*, the "lion" business is, financially, almost self-sustaining, but its manager must guard the business's competitive position at all costs to stave off any incursions on market share. Though the manager certainly cannot ignore profits, investments in new products and manufacturing technology, necessary to hold the company's competitive advantage, take precedence over short-term earnings objectives.
- **Cow.** (Low growth, high relative share) All lion businesses eventually become cash cows when growth tapers off and the relative

Relative Market Share	Market Growth	
	High	*Low*
High	II. Lion (Star)	III. Cow
Low	I. Wildcat	IV. Dog

Figure 7.2 Business-Unit Classification Model

market share of all competitors reaches equilibrium. The managers of cash cows will focus on maximizing cash flow by eliminating future-oriented investments in research and development and plant expansion, making only those investments required to maintain a competitive operating-cost structure. Vigilance to detect signs of complacency in any corner of the organization is necessary to protect against competitive initiatives that may upset the market equilibrium and transform the cash cow into a "dog."

▌**Wildcat.** (High growth, low relative share) The future lions are found among wildcat businesses, but so are the future dogs. A wildcat manager's challenge is to commit adequate funds to keep the venture on a path toward developing a market franchise that can sustain the business through the rapid-growth stage of the industry. Falling short of this objective, the manager must be decisive in scuttling the venture and cutting its losses or progressively reducing investment until a satisfactory cash flow can no longer be attained.

▌**Dog.** (Low growth, low relative share) Many managers spend far too much time trying to transform dogs or disguise their pedigrees as the wildcats of the future. These businesses usually have little real strategic value and are most often earmarked for divestiture, but they can occasionally be resurrected through downsizing and niche marketing. Through either of these transitions—turnaround or predivestiture "scrubbing"—management must not lose its zeal in scrutinizing any expenditure or other threat to the business's profit margins.

The failure of compensation planning to embrace these perspectives on business strategy and to match them, one for one, with compensation policies is the single most important reason for this discipline's current isolation and subservient disposition. A reader who wishes to take issue with this conclusion need only turn to Peters and Waterman (in their best-selling *In Search of Excellence*) who said, "The genius of pay-for-performance is not in the concept or the tools, but in the execution," and that "adaptive management is the key, and the tools and reward systems (merely) follow in top management's zig-zagging footsteps." With an epitaph like this for their discipline, it is improbable that planners will reclaim their credibility unless they first develop a working knowledge of business strategy and then translate this strategy into succinct compensation policies that strengthen accountability up and down the organization.

Models for the Middle

Until now, we have discussed strategy models almost exclusively in the context of a business unit with profit-and-loss, as well as balance-sheet, accountability; and by implication, these strategy models would be prescriptive of compensation policy only for a senior-executive group. Closer examination reveals that these paradigms can also be effective in classifying some of the middle-management performance units (see chapter 4) and in guiding the design of incentive programs for the product- and account-management teams that cut across organizational boundaries. In fact, incentive compensation can play a key role in creating cohesion within these teams where provincial interests would otherwise tend to dominate.

Although the strategic models themselves are once again the basis for classification (Figure 7.3), the roles of middle managers are different enough from those of senior managers to warrant further investigation:

▮ **Rainmaker.** (Manages high-growth, high-relative-share business segment) Product lines or major accounts from which the company expects rapid growth and major contributions to profitability are the lion cubs on the middle-management plain. Although market conditions have attained some level of stability as a frame of ref-

Relative Market Share	Market Growth	
	High	*Low*
High	Lion II. Rainmaker	Cow III. Caretaker
Low	Wildcat I. Gunslinger	Dog IV. Surfer

Figure 7.3 Performance-Unit Classification Model

erence for the rainmaker's accountabilities, this manager must continually challenge the status quo and seed the clouds of change in the hopes of creating a strengthened market position or improving profitability. Convention should not inhibit the rainmaker, and final success is measured more by the number of new avenues that are explored than by the incremental results derived from any single avenue.

▌**Caretaker.** (Manages low-growth, high-relative-share business segment) Cash calves are the product and account equivalents of their maternal business units. Managers involved with these kinds of low-risk activities are often cast in a deprecatory light. However, these managers are usually charged with guarding the market positions and preserving the financial welfare of an important and well-established piece of the company's business. Above all, the compensation planner must guard against any attempt to disguise the role of caretakers as something more aggressive, which in turn could lead to cost escalation and incongruous management behavior.

▌**Gunslinger.** (Manages high-growth, low-relative-share business segment) A scarce few large corporations have been successful in isolating enclaves of innovation and entrepreneurship within the confines of their organizational hierarchies. The risks associated with digressing from a traditional career path and casting one's lot with a wildcat venture are usually overriding impediments to the formation of these "subcultures." Where these attempts have been successful, the managers of wildcat ventures usually favor action and reaction over planning and analysis. Their role is to search out and exploit market vulnerabilities and to improvise solutions when the existing organization is too slow to act. (This topic will be covered in greater detail in the last section of this chapter.)

∎ **Surfer.** (Manages low-growth, low-relative-share business segment) It is rare to find the account or product-line equivalent of a business-unit dog, since it is hard to justify dedicating middle-management resources to a product or account group in its final stages of decline. Nonetheless, it is not unusual to find mature but still viable pieces of a company's business that are necessary, but unattractive, middle-management accountabilities. (Usually, these are unattractive because they are low-margin and/or highly cyclical businesses.) Successful managers of these product lines or accounts must in essence stand upright on a thin plank while riding the crests and troughs of a rough sea. Readiness and the ability to react quickly to changing conditions with a flexibly designed organization and production system are the fundamentals of success in this environment. In many ways, then, surfers are similar to gunslingers; the primary difference is that gunslingers are riding the crest of a wave whereas surfers are paddling against a strong undertow.

The compensation planner should not assume with this middle-management model that all performance units within a business will fall into a single cell of the classification matrix. In fact, it is quite likely that a sizable or diverse business unit would have market or product-management positions that fall into all four of the cells. In these cases, the organization is susceptible to internal competition on at least two fronts—personal stature and organization resources. So to allay this sometimes destructive, but natural, form of competition, the compensation planner must be careful not to confuse equity with equality.

The reader may recall that this is not the first time we have warned compensation planners of the pitfalls of a synonymous interpretation of equity and equality. When we discussed pay risk, several arguments were offered for an eclectic assignment of risk levels to positions up and down the organization rather than the symmetrical matching of risk to the organization's horizontal layers. Now, as we look at the weighting of performance measures and the width of the payable performance range, it should be clear that equity—allowing for policy variations to fit the business—rather than equality should guide the planner in designing incentive plans for positions that have similar responsibilities but are in different lines of business.

The Compensation Connection

After following a rather circuitous route through the strategic animal kingdom, in this section we prescribe compensation-policy guidelines for four distinct groups of managers. For the first two groups, senior and middle managers, the classifications outlined previously have very specific incentive-plan design implications. The third group, described as outliers in chapter 4, includes senior-level human resources, financial, operations, and technical managers. The final group is made up of supervisors and other nonmanagerial workers. The strategy classifications for these latter two categories of employees provide less-specific but equally useful guidelines for setting compensation policy.

Senior/Middle Management

Archetypal management-incentive plans combine financial and nonfinancial performance measures, and they reward managers for results in a range of 80% to 120% of the target, or budget. Unfortunately, two important incentive-plan features—performance-measure mix and payout range—are almost always dictated by management intuition and sometimes even management bravado (for example, "We won't pay for anything below our targets!"). Although there is a role for management know-how and intuition in weighting performance measures and setting the width of payout ranges, there is also an opportunity to enhance this intuitive product with a firm business-management rationale.

Payout Ranges

The strategy classifications are first used to provide guidelines to set the boundaries of the acceptable performance range, as illustrated in Figure 7.4. A close look at the nature of performance units, or companies, in each of the strategy classes reveals a wide variation in the precision of objective setting and the scope of management prerogative. These realities in turn dictate the width of the payable performance range as described here:

Cell I. In a new business or in one that is struggling to survive, there is an absence of meaningful performance history as a foundation for objective setting; consequently, the acceptable range of performance should

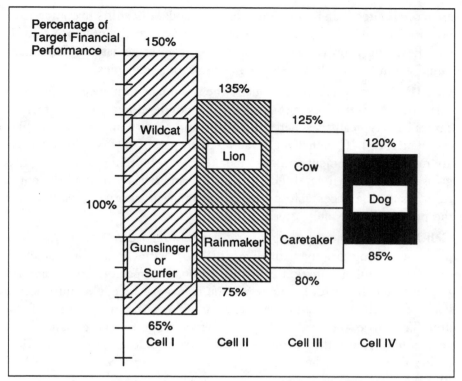

Figure 7.4 Incentive-Performance Range: Relationship to Strategy Stage

be quite broad to accommodate the imprecision of the planning process and to yield payout schedules with gradual slopes. This should not be interpreted to mean that management will exhibit tolerance of substandard performance or that it will readily accept excuses for missed targets. On the contrary, unable to accurately forecast financial results, management will be preoccupied with the thresholds of performance that define commercial viability (for example, sales revenue growth, key customer acquisition, customer traffic, production quality) and with the affordability of incentive payments above these thresholds.

Cell II. Companies or performance units in this high-growth stage have established a position in their industry and are trying to build market share and diversify their customer base. Formalized annual planning usually shapes management's expectations for the business. Thus, the acceptable performance range is narrower and management's prerogatives are more limited than in the Cell I start-up mode. But shifts in competitive position and swings in industry cycles can unexpectedly influence results, and these uncertainties dictate the use of an intermediate performance-range width and moderate slopes in the payout schedules.

Cell III. Industry cycles are usually the dominant influence on the performance of enterprises in this mature stage of development, since market shares have typically reached equilibrium and other competitive variables are neutralized. The challenges facing managers of this type of business are margin management and customer relations. Incremental competitive gains are highly visible, difficult to obtain, and usually of modest scope. As a result, the acceptable performance range is relatively narrow, but the payout slope is quite steep.

Cell IV. Management prerogative is severely restricted when dog companies are being groomed for divestiture. Priorities focus on protection of an asset—either a market franchise or financial-performance stability. If a favorable divestiture is achieved, the manager's incentive must not be confused with that of an investment banker negotiating the sale of the unit. Therefore, the acceptable performance range for these managers is very confined, and the payout is usually fixed (unless there is a participation provision for the manager to share in the proceeds of the divestiture).

Performance-Measure Mix

The blend of financial performance measures (for example, earnings or return on investment) and strategic milestones (that is, nonfinancial objectives) is the second incentive-plan design issue influenced by a unit's strategy classification. The critical question is how much weight the financial-performance measures should carry. And once again the strategy categories used in determining performance ranges lead to analogous conclusions regarding performance-measure mix (see Figure 7.5). Whereas planning precision and industry stability were dominant influences in setting the ranges, management prerogative is the controlling factor for weighting the financial-performance measures.

Cell I. Managers charged with building a business in a start-up or turn-around mode are usually given broad decision-making authority and must look beyond a single year's results in forming a strategic perspective. Consequently, annual financial measures carry the least weight in these managers' incentive plans, and programmatic market-development initiatives are given the most attention.

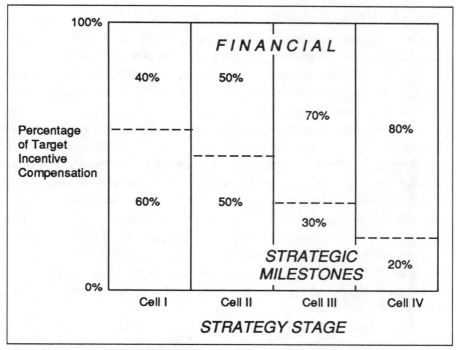

Figure 7.5 Performance-Measure Mix: Relationship to Strategy Stage

Cell II. Growth is contributory only in the context of acceptable financial return. Therefore, in this stage the mix of performance measures shifts to emphasize more heavily the concrete financial expectations for the enterprise.

Cell III. The essential role of a cash cow (or calf) is simply to generate a consistent financial return. Changes in direction or major capital investments are rare, and the managers are charged primarily with harvesting the business by maintaining a steady course and keeping a watchful eye on competitive threats. Performance standards therefore tend to concentrate on one or two key financial dimensions and provide for very selective highlighting of strategic initiatives.

Cell IV. The manager of a company being divested will have the least latitude to alter the course of the business or its asset base. Thus, the focus of this manager's performance standards is almost exclusively on preserving cash flow and safeguarding short-term financial performance.

The Outliers

The financial, human resources, operations, engineering, and other support functions are frequently refugees of the incentive-plan design process. As discussed in chapter 4, some of these managers who are dedicated to a business unit or product/account group may find a natural home, whereas others remain out in the cold.

Compensation planners commonly treat outliers by arbitrarily including them in incentive plans designed for core participants, acknowledging that the unique contributions of these staff functions are difficult to isolate and measure in their own right. The rationale for including these functions in incentive programs therefore has less to do with influencing the supportive behavior of these managers than it does with a desire to achieve homogeneity (under the guise of equity) across the management ranks. With the business strategy categories introduced in this chapter, it is now possible to resolve the questions left unanswered in chapter 4 regarding outlier participation in company incentive plans, as illustrated in Figure 7.6.

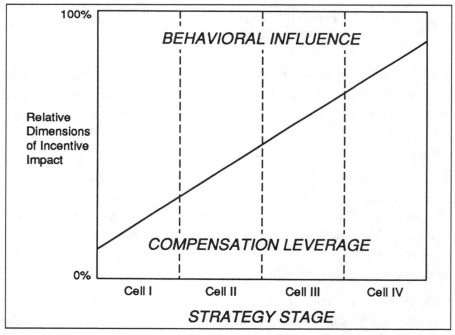

Figure 7.6 Impact of Incentives on Outliers: Relationship to Strategy Stage

Cells I and II Implications. In these high growth stages of development, it is desirable to reinforce a collegial spirit among the management team members, because mutual trust and shared values are the forerunners of individual initiative. In a software-development company funded by venture capital, the grooming of the company for its initial public offering was management's dominant focus. But before this objective could be accomplished, success in building the internal organization and an external market presence were hand-in-glove prerequisites. The staff of this organization, whether technical programmers, accountants, or lawyers, were vital contributors to the company's success because of their roles in structuring customer contracts or supporting software installations.

To create an artificial compensation barrier that would allow only the management group to "hear the bell" when it rings for the acquisition of a major new customer or for the successful trial run of a new system would have been destructive to the cohesion of this organization. The incentive program that was installed first granted each employee a limited number of shares in the company and then assigned all employees to one or more teams that worked toward specific goals. Incentives were paid for the accomplishment of the goals, and the amounts paid were increased or decreased based on the company's overall performance. With this system of incentives, the company was able to accomplish a combination of motivational objectives: to reinforce individual or group accountability and to intensify the employees' sense of sharing in the entire company's success.

Cells III and IV Implications. The lines of demarcation between line and staff functions are pronounced in these latter stages of the life cycle, and the staff roles are dominated by maintenance and administrative activities. The inclusion of the outliers in an incentive program during these stages will certainly serve the cause of leveraging compensation, but the behavioral impact of a program is eroded by the clear separation of line and staff responsibilities.

Take, for example, the controller of a $300 million multidivision manufacturing company who participates in a senior-management bonus plan that is tied primarily to the company's achievement of its profit objectives. A small portion of this bonus is also tied to his accomplishment of some personal objectives. A similar program encompasses the legal and human resources managers, not only the department heads but also the middle managers in these functions. When we reviewed this program with the managers, it became clear that although they did not complain about their bonus payments, they unanimously acknowledged their narrow influence on the financial results that drove the program. This disconnection, though benign when company performance was good, had the potential to disgruntle this group of employees in times of weaker performance.

Though it is unlikely that a universal formula for gauging the impact of company performance-based incentives on outlier positions can be defined, the general relationship indicated in Figure 7.6 is probably accurate in most situations. As a business matures and becomes more functionally organized, and as the sheer number of employees grows, the line of sight between bottom-line performance and individual contribution becomes murky. Thus, the impact of these broad-based incentives moves gradually out of the behavioral realm and more into that of financial leverage. And as this transformation progresses, caution must be exercised to prevent the "incentive" plan from becoming a predator on the morale of the company.

The Third Estate

Most first-line supervisors and members of the nonmanagerial work force are disenfranchised from participation in a company's incentive plans, except occasionally when gain-sharing programs comprehensively cover the employee population. In these exceptional instances, the compensation planner justifies the program by citing its supporting role in reinforcing an essential cultural value such as teamwork. The impact of the programs on individual performance or employee behavior tends to be a secondary consideration, and the concept of compensation risk (see chapter 5) at these levels in the organization is not a prominent policy concern.

Again, if the compensation objective is to provide a true incentive to the organization's third estate, business strategy and the stage in the life cycle should not be ignored. Regardless of the program's cultural intent, the strategy classifications should serve as a guide to anticipate gain-sharing's behavioral impact.

In the early start-up or high-growth stages, where the employee's line of sight to the business unit's results is unobstructed, gain-sharing incentives can create excitement, camaraderie, and a constructive sense of urgency that supports management's direction. However, in the latter stages of the life cycle, management's prerogatives are constrained, and broad-based incentives tend to follow the general welfare of the company. At the same time, the line of sight to the unit's results is obscured by the growing bureaucracy. So, unless compensation is truly at risk (that is, base salaries for these employees are below competitive levels), there is a high probability that gain-sharing programs will add a permanent layer of cost, produce little in the way of permanent productivity enhancement, and further erode margins at a time when margins are uppermost on management's list of priorities.

If, on the other hand, there is a clear perception of compensation risk within the third-estate group of employees, the incentive plan can have a powerful impact on productivity and cost control. The history of incentive design for this group of employees is replete with examples that are strongly supportive as well as those that are horrifying. As we noted previously, at this level incentives are interpreted literally. With that interpretation comes a risk that any message communicated through the incentive program that is not precisely in tune with management's intent can produce results that are drastically counter to that intent. Briefly stated, incentives for the third estate are in many cases practical and productive; the line between productive and disastrous, however, is thin and grey.

Captive New-Venture Managers

As independent enterprises, new ventures and start-up (or even turn-around) companies pose several policy issues that to a large degree have already been addressed in our discussion of the compensation implications for Cell I (wildcat) business units. However, when these types of units find themselves surrounded by the sometimes smothering attention of a larger corporate parent, the compensation policy issues take on a different hue.

When large corporations attempt the internal development of a fledgling business, their strongest, but often fatal, impulse is to mold the unit in the image of the corporation, adopting the familiar accoutrements of the corporation's mature businesses as necessities for the venture. Though it is true that the support services (accounting, recruitment, legal, occupancy, and so forth) supplied by the corporation provide an unequivocal advantage over a grass-roots start-up, the venture must have a realistic sense of the true costs of these services to accurately assess its performance as a stand-alone entity.

Moreover, the venture must avoid excessive use of the corporation's freely dispensed services to ensure that the rigidity of corporate standards does not paralyze the venture's decision-making processes. Although it is difficult for corporate management to switch gears and accept the nonconformity of the new-venture world, it is equally difficult for the venture-management team to turn off the spigot of corporate services once they have begun to flow. Whether or not the venture absorbs the costs of the support services and other niceties, both corporate and venture management must guard against an overabundance of these frills that would undermine the "hungry rat" psychology essential to a new venture's viability.

The Culture Club

"Culture" has been overbilled as a watchword for new-venture success inside large corporations. But to submit that all will be well if only the new venture is permitted to act as an independent start-up company is cold comfort to a corporate management concentrated on the next quarter's bottom line. The challenge, then, is to find a management formula that neither bridles the success of the new venture nor weakens the control of the corporation. In searching for this formula, though, corporate management is more likely to treat the venture as an analogue of the project-management process. On the surface, this seems like a practical solution, but if a new venture is viewed as just another MBO (management by objectives) for a senior manager, it is destined to fail on at least three fronts:

■ **Building Stand-Alone Market Value.** Corporate "projects" rarely aim at building stand-alone market value. A new venture, on the other hand, must be viewed from the beginning as if its existence depends on funding by independent investors. The investor may judge the value of a business on criteria other than sales and profitability. This value can encompass such business basics as market franchise, long-term diversification opportunities, unique management expertise, and a clear progression in financial performance.

Although these nonfinancial performance bench marks are often the most important indicators of a venture's commercial viability in its early years, rarely do these indicators carry sufficient weight with corporate management to mitigate its instinctive emphasis on short-term financial results. And without a focus on market value, the stage is set for management to concentrate on current financial results and to be caught in an endless cycle of short-interval (go/

no-go) decision making that will enervate the venture's management team.

■ **Understanding Performance Imperatives.** A new enterprise can tolerate few false starts. Therefore, management must have a firm and unwavering grasp of the underlying factors essential to the venture's success and it must build the organization with a single-minded dedication to these factors. Despite this mandate, corporate management tends to look inward for guidance in designing a new venture's organization and compensation structure and in setting its strategic priorities. This perspective leads to the creation of jobs that primarily accommodate individual capacities and conform to conventional divisions of responsibility. More critically, this thinking also leads management to dwell on analysis and market definition rather than on the distillation of a few essential conclusions that can form the foundation of the venture's performance imperatives.

■ **Managing New-Venture Careers.** Forming the new-venture management team is almost always a study in compromise—compromise that is struck primarily between the *desired* talents and those available (willing and able) to assume a new-venture role. It is natural for management to look inside the corporation for star performers. But stars have usually been created using the yardstick of corporate values, and these values are often quite different from those required for success in the venture. Furthermore, these managers are frequently recruited under the misguided premise that a return to the corporate mainstream is a viable future option. In reality, though, the independence and scope of responsibility these managers enjoy in their venture positions is frequently in conflict with a traditional corporate career path.

In its attempt to attract the stars to a new venture, management will often provide continued benefits, compensation, and organizational stature as an enticement. And there is often an implicit guarantee of job security if the venture is unsuccessful. Unfortunately, these promises are neither realistic nor supportive of the new-venture concept. Transferring corporate personnel policies and programs to the new venture, even for its senior management, fails to acknowledge the cost characteristics and competitive pressures of the fledgling enterprise. Moreover, although some quid pro quo is appropriate to offset the manager's inherent career risks, the candidacy of any individual who is overly concerned with these "life-as-usual" amenities is of questionable merit.

The Valence of New Ventures

Valence is a term chemists use to describe the combining capacity of a group of atoms. It is also a term that has applicability in describing the capacity of the members of a new-venture management team to combine their forces in launching a new business and carving out a permanent market franchise. To catalyze this "reaction," compensation and organization must come together in a formula that integrates two well-tested venture-management principles:

1. **Mutual Trust and Shared Risks within the Venture-Management Team.** The ground rules for personal success shift dramatically for a manager in a corporate venture. Individual accomplishments are displaced by a new barometer—the commercial viability of the total business. For this shift to be embraced by the new-venture management team, the organizational structure must mandate the sharing of accountabilities across all functional lines. Such a partnership can be realized only when all senior managers

   ▎ are "in the loop" in building customer relationships,

   ▎ have access to key resources that is unencumbered by organizational bureaucracy, and

   ▎ are involved in line decisions irrespective of their primary staff or line responsibilities.

2. **Financial Rewards Linked to Critical Commercial Viability Bench Marks.** For incentive compensation to have real value, it must simulate equity participation for the key management group. In this context, the manager's equity value should be tied to separate measures of performance that reflect the following:

   ▎ **Milestones on the Way to Commercial Viability.** The organizational philosophy suggested above prescribed the dilution of the traditional functional reporting structure to create a strong management team. In contrast, the performance-measurement system, particularly in the early stages of the venture's development, must concentrate on functional progress exclusively. Thus, achievements with key customers, product technology, operations, or manufacturing should be the primary focal points for an annual bonus program.

■ **The Market Value of the Business.** The financial-performance measures for a new venture change as it progresses through its own life cycle. At first, with the venture's priorities focused on establishing credibility in the marketplace, sales and other top-line indicators are the relevant yardsticks for the venture's management team. Later on, the performance measures gravitate toward profitability and related balance-sheet ratios. Building market value, therefore, is not just a short-term, one-dimensional proposition—it results from compounding all of the management team's judgments in making financial and operational trade-offs during the venture's progress toward viability.

The benefits of making intelligent trade-offs can be clearly recognized when a longer-term incentive element acts as a counterbalance to the annual bonus program. With a fully integrated compensation program that links annual "dividends" to commercial viability bench marks and long-term payouts to a financial composite that represents market value (or "share appreciation"), the venture company can be managed with the perspective of an outside investor.

At this point, the message should be clear that there are important distinctions between the role of a small-company manager and that of an entrepreneur/investor. Although new ventures under the aegis of a large corporation require an entrepreneurial perspective, it is usually impractical to provide direct investment opportunities for the venture's management team. Thus, organization and compensation must be used creatively to reinforce clear functional performance milestones while supporting an organizational structure that only nominally depends on functional definition. To make these elements converge, corporate managers must adopt a new performance-management vocabulary, and the venture managers must exercise a unifying leadership style that cements accountabilities that are shared through the organization.

8

Incentive Engineering

Springloading the Message

An incentive plan's impact on participants is only as great as the clarity and power of its message. In the preceding chapters we have shaped a new language with which to deliver the message, stripping away the barnacles of conventional practice from the now-familiar spokes of the compensation-policy wheel—incentive eligibility, compensation mix, performance measurement, and internal equity. In this penultimate step toward rounding out the wheel, we explore the mechanical structure of incentive plans to seek out ways in which simple arithmetic can be used to amplify management's directional messages.

Once again, conventional practice (in this case with its nose ring attached to the KISS principle) should be viewed skeptically by the compensation policymaker. As ludicrous as it would be to put a Yugo engine in a luxury Mercedes-Benz sedan, it would be equally out of place to have spent all of this effort on business and organization analysis only to apply a simple, linear payout schedule to two or three carefully chosen performance criteria. The challenge ahead, then, is to uncover the management trade-offs embedded in the performance criteria and to enhance the visibility of these decisions through the creative "calculus" of the payout structure.

Dissecting the Payout Curve

The bottom line of any incentive program is the relationship between a payout amount and a performance level. An incentive program's payout schedule is the usual means of communicating this relationship to the participant (for example, an employee is paid 90 percent of target incentive for achieving 90 percent of the target performance). However, a simple, linear progression of payouts matched to an identical progression in performance may ignore important realities regarding the imprecision and uncertainty surrounding a company's objective-setting process. And through these omissions, areas of under- and overpayment in the payout schedule can be created.

As noted in chapters 6 and 7, the incentive plan should recognize the uncertainty of the business environment by graduating payouts through the full breadth of the acceptable performance range from minimum acceptable to maximum payable. In addition, if one accepts that the planning process is at best a probabilistic exercise and that actual results will approximate a normal (bell-shaped) distribution around the target (that is, the probability of results is highest near the target and tapers off in either direction, see Figure 8.1) rather than a uniform distribution where all results have the same probability, then the use of a linear payout formula to span the performance range is of questionable value.

Instead, the conventional straight-line payout schedule should be twisted at the tails of the normal distribution to better match payments to the real difficulty of achieving incremental results and to thereby enhance the motivational value of the plan. This "anguine" (snake-shaped) payout structure is illustrated in Figure 8.2, and its unique anatomy is dissected in the following paragraphs.

The Payout Threshold

The first distinction of this payout structure is that payments are made at performance levels *below* the target, starting at a minimum acceptable threshold of performance. Senior management will often question the use of incentives in this range, but assuming that pay is actually at risk in the incentive program, these same managers should be concerned about the competitiveness of their *total* compensation program. If a manager is unduly penalized for performance slightly below a target because of a precipitous curtailment of incentive payments in that range of performance, it will not be long before the company becomes fertile ground for

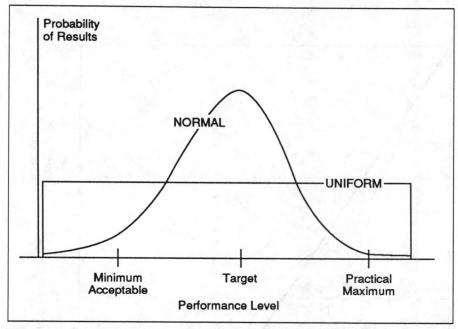

Figure 8.1 Comparison of Uniform and Normal Planning Scenarios

the predatory recruiting tactics of competitors. Thus, in setting the minimum performance threshold for incentive payments, the compensation planner should form the policy around the following three considerations:

Communicating Shared Risk. Common sense dictates that any acknowledged imprecision in the objective-setting process (for example, plus or minus 5 percent of target) be accommodated in the incentive payout schedule by paying near target amounts for performance within the planning precision range of the objective. (Any other payout approach reduces real opportunity in the plan and postures the program more as simple gain sharing, in which only surplus earnings are distributed.) Although participants' total compensation may still fall short of competitive levels, even when payouts are scheduled below target performance, a perception of sharing compensation risk between the company and the individual employee will go a considerable distance in protecting the motivational message of the program and in reducing capricious personnel turnover.

Fortifying the Incentive Premise. Beyond this risk-sharing consideration, there is yet a more fundamental question raised by those who would prohibit incentive payments below 100 percent of goal. An attitude that

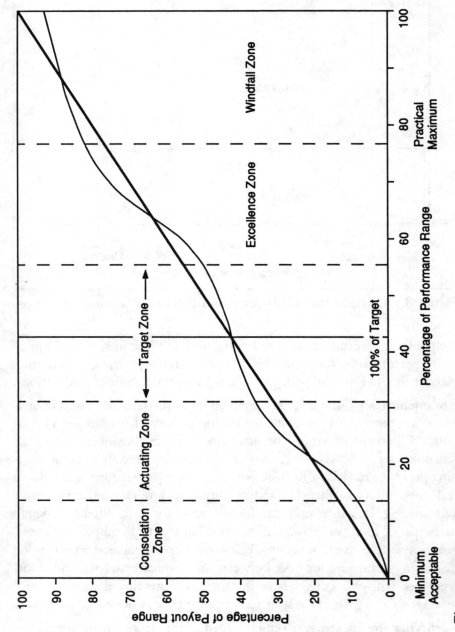

Figure 8.2 The Anguine Payout Curve

staunchly resists these subtarget payments is symptomatic of a profound but perhaps subconscious denial of an essential incentive premise: As participation in an incentive plan broadens and each participant's earnings appetite is whetted, the participants' overall effort to improve performance is heightened.

Recalling the assumption that performance will follow a bell-shaped probability distribution, a payout schedule that pays only for above-target performance will by definition exclude either 50 percent of the plan participants or yield a payout only 50 percent of the time. In these instances where the full span of acceptable performance is not included in the payout schedule, the credibility of an incentive plan's message is destroyed. So the compensation planner must be sensitive to the true performance range of any objective and must ensure that actual participation in an incentive program is not limited to overachievers and that participants performing in the subtarget range continue to be motivated throughout the year.

Safeguarding Planning Integrity. A knee-jerk reaction to low incentive-plan participation (for example, less than 70 percent of eligible employees receiving at least a nominal payout) is to reduce performance objectives. Similarly, if payouts from the plan seem too high, management assumes that the goals are too easily achieved and tends to raise the performance thresholds. Using the objective-setting process in this manner to modulate incentive payouts sends a signal to participants that the planning process is nothing more than a means of controlling their earnings. To avoid this insidious undermining of a crucial business discipline, compensation planners should use creative incentive-payout structures to reward for planning integrity and to ensure an equitable balance between the company's payout exposure and the individual's compensation risk.

A case in point is a manufacturer of communication and electrical components that pays division executives a bonus for achievement of a planned earnings target. In evaluating the divisional business plans, the CEO was frustrated by the tendency of these managers, who were merely exhibiting their individual management styles, to either sandbag or overstate their objectives. Wanting to protect the planning process from arbitrary "corporate" adjustments, this CEO was determined to bring greater equity into the bonus program.

To this end, he introduced an informal objective-grading process that established three separate payout curves to match his assessment of the difficulty of each division executive's objectives. This scheme, illustrated in Figure 8.3, modestly increases or decreases the payouts at each level of performance depending on the aggressiveness of the plan. So at 95 percent of target for a division operating under schedule A, the payout would be 30 percent of base salary, whereas a more aggressive manager with tougher targets operating under schedule C would receive 46 percent at the same 95 percent level of performance. Futhermore, the first manager would have to achieve over 120 percent of the target to realize this same 46 percent payout.

Having a solid grasp of the characteristics and market dynamics of each of the divisions, the CEO established his own standards of qualification for each schedule, but to guard against any specious comparison of these unlike divisions, he does not openly discuss the criteria with the managers. In another company where the business is more homogeneous, this objective-grading system can be used more openly to stretch a manager's planning horizons. For instance, the criteria for regional sales managers could be based on three preset ranges of sales growth; the highest growth rate would place a manager under schedule C and the lowest under schedule A.

Incentive Zones

The second and perhaps more radical distinction of the anguine schedule is its undulating progression through the performance range. A linear

Bonus Percentage of Base Salary

Percentage of Earnings Target Achieved	Objective Grade		
	A	B	C
75%	0%	0%	0%
80	4	5	6
85	10	12	14
90	22	27	32
95	30	38	46
100	32	40	48
105	34	42	50
110	36	45	54
115	40	50	60
120	44	55	66
125+	48	60	72

Figure 8.3 The Family of Payout Schedules

formula tells the participant that each increment in performance has the identical value at any point in the performance range. Some variations on the linear formula (especially in real estate and retail businesses) have modified this message by incorporating accelerated payments above certain thresholds, but these modifications go only part of the way toward bringing reality into the payout schedule. To fully incorporate the normal distribution premise in the schedule, the linear formula must be reshaped—not just at the top end of the curve, but along its entire span to match payout progressions to key zones of performance:

■ **Consolation Zone.** Rewards are not significant in this first segment of the payout schedule; in fact, they even fall short of awards that would be paid using a linear formula. Participants entering the plan at this level will have an inducement to move into the actuating zone where the payout progression accelerates rapidly. The company has in essence made a trade-off in the incentive structure, extending participation to lower levels of performance but reducing payments at these levels to enhance the incentive value in the actuating zone.

■ **Actuating Zone.** This segment of the curve is the launching pad of the program, providing a greater reward than the linear formula to employees who reach the target *range* of performance. Consistent with an achievement-pay philosophy, the accelerated payout progression of the actuating zone indicates that large dividends will be paid to participants for attaining standard performance, and, coincidentally, heavy penalties will be levied when performance falls short of the target range.

■ **Target Zone.** On several occasions, target performance has been discussed as a range rather than as a single number. Any straight-line payout formula must by its nature place undue emphasis on a discrete point in the schedule at which the target award is earned. Increments of performance above and below this point are treated like any others in the entire performance range. Contrastingly, the anguine schedule's progression accelerates outside the target performance range and minimizes the distinction among payouts within the immediate vicinity of the target. In this way, the imprecision of the objective-setting process is buffered, and the incentive schedule neither under- nor overpays for performance at any point in this zone.

■ **Excellence Zone.** Analogous to the actuating zone, employees who step into the realm of outstanding performance are rewarded by a steep progression in payout opportunity (that should be commensurate with the added effort required). Again, payouts near the lower boundary of the zone are less than those the linear formula would prescribe, but they are offset by much-greater payments toward the upper boundary of the zone, thereby creating the same accelerating effect of the actuating zone.

■ **Windfall Zone.** In most performance scenarios, there is a zone above the practical maximum that an employee can possibly attain, but such achievement is unpredictable because it is dependent on unusual events. Normally, it is inappropriate to pay on a proportionate basis for this type of achievement, but management should be willing to share some of the benefits from these windfalls. A sharing method suggested by the anguine schedule extends the performance progression beyond the maximum practical level and is accompanied by a similar, but very gradual, extension of the payout progression. Another approach is to truncate the anguine curve above the maximum practical level and adopt a discretionary provision in the incentive program that permits the payment of a one-time lump-sum amount—say an additional 5 percent to 10 percent of base salary—for extraordinary performance. With this kind of provision, a degree of subjectivity is introduced in favor of the fiscal control that could be lost with the first method.

A Multigoal Incentive Structure with "Teeth"

In chapter 6, we introduced an approach to gaining commitment and overcoming management skepticism regarding "programmatic" incentive goals. Even though management has agreed to meaningful goals using the guidelines prescribed in that chapter, the programmatic incentive plan may still fail management's credibility test for want of a stringent performance-measurement process and method for calibrating the payout schedule. To clear this hurdle, the objective must be coupled with measurement and payout structures that reward for balanced attention to all goals and that force a decisive evaluation of results.

Using orthodox, open-ended payout schedules for the multigoal system of incentives usually rewards managers for the accomplishment of each goal *independently* and communicates the relative importance of the goals by varying target bonus amounts. An example of this type of program is illustrated in Figure 8.4. Though this structure is straightforward, it imposes no constraints on how managers spend their time. They may choose to trade off overachievement on one objective for inattention to another and in the process still earn a target bonus. The messages of this structure are contradictory in that they state plainly that "standard" performance does not embody a requirement for balancing the priorities inherent in the multigoal plan.

Another feature of the orthodox payout scheme is the use of continuous scales for measuring performance. Although the anguine payout schedule is excellent for broad financial and operations performance measures, its use in the programmatic arena is limiting. When a company

Position: Plant manager   **Target bonus: 30% of base salary**

Objectives
1. Increase plant productivity to at least $11.50 in value added per man-hour.
2. Reduce lost-time accidents to at least 15 minutes per 1,000 man-hours worked.
3. Increase raw materials and work-in-process inventory turns to at least 5.2 times.

Objective Weighting/Bonus Allocation		
Objective	Weighting	Bonus Allocation (% of Base Salary)
Plant productivity	50%	15%
Lost-time accident rate	30	9
Inventory turns	20	6

Payout Schedules					
Plant Productivity		Lost-Time Accidents		Inventory Turns	
Performance Level	Payout	Performance Level	Payout	Performance Level	Payout
$10.50	0%	25 min.	0%	4.5X	0%
11.00	5	20	3	4.9	2
11.50	15	15	9	5.2	6
12.00	18	11	11	5.6	8
12.50	25	7	15	6.0	10

Figure 8.4 An Orthodox Multigoal Incentive Structure

judges achievement of programmatic goals, it is frequently as important to assess *how* the goals were attained as it is to measure the degree of attainment. Few companies would feel comfortable paying incentives to managers for accomplishing programmatic goals if priorities were not balanced well or if other important job accountabilities were neglected. The incentive structure must therefore provide management with a means to modulate the hard voice of "results" with a softer voice that qualitatively assesses tactics.

The structures illustrated in Figures 8.5 and 8.6 introduce a system that integrates several performance goals and uses discrete categories to force unequivocal performance evaluation. These structures, along with the features described in the following text, will help compensation planners clear the final hurdle of management skepticism by tightening the controls on payouts and clearing up the message to managers.

Discrete Performance Steps

The study of the anguine curve's anatomy reveals three primary zones of performance in which incentive payments accelerate or decelerate. Similarly, this multigoal framework incorporates three performance grades: minimum acceptable, meeting expectations, and outstanding. In

Position: *Plant manager*		*Target bonus: 30%*
Objective		**Basis of Measurement**
Increase plant productivity Reduce lost-time accidents Improve working-capital utilization		Value added per man-hour Lost time per 1,000 man-hours WIP and material inventory turnover
Objective Weighting and Performance-Level Definition		
Minimum Acceptable	**Meeting Expectations**	**Outstanding**
Objective: Productivity improvement (Weight: 50%)		
$10.50–$11.35	$11.25–$12.10	Above $12.00
Objective: Lost-time accidents (Weight: 30%)		
25 min.–18 min.	19 min.–13 min.	Less than 14 min.
Objective: Inventory turns (Weight: 20%)		
4.5X–5.0X	4.9X–5.5X	Above 5.4X

Figure 8.5 The Composite Multigoal Incentive Structure

Objective	Weight	Performance Rating			Weighted Performance Rating
		Minimum Acceptable	Meeting Expectations	Outstanding	
Plant productivity	50%	15	50	75	50
Lost-time accidents	30%	9	30	45	9
Inventory turns	20%	6	20	30	30
Totals	100%	30	100	150	89

Incentive-Payout Schedule		
Performance Rating Points	Percentage of Target Bonus Paid	Actual Bonus (Based on 30% Target)
Less than 45	0%	0%
60	20	6
75	60	18
90	80	24
100	100	30
110	120	36
125	150	45
140	170	51
150	200	60

Figure 8.6 Composite Performance Profile and Payout Schedule

this format, however, the payouts do not follow a continuous progression but advance in discrete steps from one performance grade to the next.

To adopt this structure, management must accept the premise that in the realm of programmatic objectives, balanced allocation of effort leading to consistent performance across all fronts is more important than incremental gains on any single front. Accordingly, the discrete performance grades shown in Figure 8.5 are expressed as ranges or brackets of performance (akin to the target zone of the anguine curve), and these brackets overlap to allow management a degree of discretion in grading performance that lies near the boundaries of any zone.

Although many scales for appraising programmatic-objective performance splinter into as many as ten levels of achievement, such hair splitting reduces performance measurement to a study in compromise and negotiation and sets the stage for a renewal of management's programmatic-objective skepticism. In stark contrast, with only three performance grades, management can be precise in defining and communicating criteria for each grade and can unequivocally defend a performance rating at the time of payout.

Composite Performance Rating

As noted earlier, when multiple goals are used in an incentive program, it is essential that the relative importance and inconvertibility of each goal is clearly conveyed by the program's structure. Using the composite-performance profile illustrated in Figure 8.6, each objective is weighted so that the sum of the weights is 100. For performance in the meeting-expectations range, the performance-rating points earned are synonymous with the weights. But to reinforce a balanced effort on each objective and to minimize the potential for outstanding achievement on one objective to fully offset weaker performance on another, the rating point spread between the minimum-acceptable and meeting-expectations performance grades must be about one and one-half times the spread between the meeting-expectations and outstanding grades. The composite-performance rating in the example is 89, which in turn is the basis for the determination of incentive payouts as illustrated in the incentive-payout schedule shown in Figure 8.6.

Looking more closely at the composite-performance results, we assume that the plant manager (1) was rated at the meeting-expectations level on the plant productivity goal (contributing 50 points to the performance profile); (2) achieved only a minimum-acceptable rating on the lost-time goal (9 points contributed); and (3) performed at the outstanding level on the inventory turn goal (earning 30 more points). In total, the composite rating of 89 still falls slightly short of the target and would earn the manager a bonus, according to the payout schedule, of about 24 percent of base salary (by interpolation).

Self-Regulating Priorities

If the performance brackets for each grade and objective in the profile are well defined, then the manager has a real-time index for adjusting priorities and focusing effort throughout the year. In a practical sense, managers will continuously read their progress on each objective and will make decisions for each of three performance scenarios:

■ **Near the Peak of a Performance Bracket.** In expectation of reaching the next higher plateau, the manager will probably choose to exert extra effort on this objective to ensure that he or she exceeds the threshold that is close at hand.

▮ **Near the Bottom of a Performance Bracket.** The risk of dropping to the next-lower plateau precipitously will probably initiate a defensive effort to protect against any further erosion of the bonus potential.

▮ **In the Middle of a Bracket.** Without a realistic hope of attaining the next-higher plateau and lacking a significant risk of falling to the lower plateau, the manager is most likely to direct attention to other more pressing objectives in hopes of balancing overall performance and perhaps exceeding a threshold for one of the other objectives.

The Power of Compound Incentives

Like the donkey who starved to death between two bales of hay, unable to make up its mind which one to eat, multigoal incentive programs can confuse a manager's sense of priorities and prompt an ad hoc and personal interpretation of an incentive plan's true intent. So the compensation planner should be keenly aware that when multiple goals are used in an incentive structure, they must sometimes be closely intertwined to directly acknowledge the interaction of certain performance dimensions and to preempt any confusion of management priorities. For instance, in a marketing organization, sales and profitability are interactive. Profit dollars can be increased in either of two ways: growth in sales at the current profit margin percentage, or increasing the margin percentage with sales held constant. If sales and profitability goals are tied to separate and independent incentive schedules, it is possible for managers to escape the natural interaction between the performance dimensions and give little attention to whichever is the more difficult task. On the other hand, if the two dimensions are inextricably blended in the payout structure, the managers have to balance their attention between the two objectives. Any other course of action will lead to subpar performance and below-target-incentive payouts.

A geometric, or compounding, relationship between the payout schedules of one performance measure and another (as illustrated in Figure 8.7) dramatically communicates the balancing act inherent in interactive incentive components. In this scheme, the base bonus is paid to a manager who achieves the sales growth target and the compounding bonus, which

Position: Vice president sales and marketing   *Target bonus: 30%*
Incentive objectives:

■ Growth in sales by 10%   ■ Gross margin of 32%

Target bonus allocation:

■ 67% sales growth   ■ 33% gross margin

Incentive Payout Structure

Sales Growth		Gross Margin	
Percentage Growth Rate	Bonus % of Base Salary	Gross Margin Percentage	Bonus % of Sales Growth Incentive Earnings
Less than 5%	0%	Less than 25%	0
6	4	26	10
7	9	28	30
9	18	30	45
10	20	32	50
12	22	34	55
14	25	36	65
16	27	38	80
18	28	40	90
20	30	42	100

Figure 8.7 Compounding Incentive Payouts

is expressed as a *percentage of the base bonus earnings*, is paid for the gross margin goal. This structure states emphatically that sales growth is important but only if it is achieved profitably. And to ensure that this message is consistent throughout the practical performance range, the construction of these schedules must adhere to the following guidelines:

Select a Core Objective. One objective (in the Figure 8.7 example, the sales growth target) should be the fulcrum in the incentive structure, whereas others—the compounding elements—should serve as constant reminders of the trade-offs the manager must make in achieving the core objective. Trade-offs other than growth and profitability can also be embodied in this type of structure and might include a two-dimensional competition between productivity (or cost) and quality as well as more complex interactions involving three or more variables.

The concept of a core objective, though, is mandatory if more than two interactive goals are used, since the interaction may not be mutual to all goals and may be relevant only to the core objective. As an example, the core objective for a sales and marketing executive might be total sales volume. In addition, some key account profitability and new product launch objectives might be incorporated in the compounding incentive structure. These latter two objectives, though distinctly related to the sales goal, do not necessarily contribute to each other. So, in placing the sales-volume objective at the core, the manager is focused on this goal as the source of leverage in the incentive program: The higher the sales volume, the more the subordinate goals are worth, regardless of the performance level on these goals. Moreover, it is evident that incremental results related to either of the subordinate goals contributes to the core objective.

Just for a contrast, consider the use of either the account-profitability or the product-launch objectives as the core. The leverage would shift to one of these new goals, but the message would be confusing. The strategic relationship between the product-launch and key-account objectives is not obvious, regardless of which of the two is at the core; and the advantage of the compounding incentive is lost.

As a final note on core objectives, the compensation planner should be encouraged to extend this concept as business priorities dictate to include "nesting" relationships among three or four compounding performance objectives. For example, suppose that a telemarketer is paid a base incentive expressed as a percentage of revenue generated. Management feels it is also important to ensure that the telemarketer continues to make calls even after achieving a daily quota. An incentive premium (that is, a percentage of the base incentive earnings) might be paid for the achievement of this objective. Management also wants the telemarketing groups to focus on a total department sales objective, which would thereby create a healthy peer pressure and stimulate supportive team behavior. A second premium could be paid as a percentage of the combined base incentive *and* call activity premium for the achievement of a monthly department quota. With this type of premium, the rewards for total-department achievement would automatically accrue to those making the strongest individual contributions to the department's success, and the message of individual and group accountability for performance is expressly stated.

Watch the Weights. With a compounding incentive structure, all goals can be weighted (as contributors to the total target-incentive payout) to fit the company's strategic priorities. Because of the compounding effects, however, it is crucial to pinpoint target and ceiling dollar payments for each objective during the design phase and then calculate the compounding percentage relationships that will achieve these payout levels.

Referring back to Figure 8.7, the weighting between the two goals at target performance is two-thirds/one-third. The payout schedule, however, has been carefully constructed to meet predefined payout targets. At the maximum of both scales, the combined payout is 60 percent of base salary—the 30 percent core bonus plus the 100 percent premium on the core bonus that is paid for achievement of the highest gross margin level. With this structure, the manager must perform well above the target and achieve 20 percent sales growth to earn a *target* bonus (30 percent of base salary) if the gross margin level drops below the 25 percent minimum threshold. (A variation on this theme might provide for a further factoring of the sales growth bonus schedule if the margin drops below this minimum threshold. This discounting could be effected by payment of only 80 percent of the scheduled bonus under these conditions.)

The relationship between the core and booster scales is also an important consideration. Setting the maximum payout on the core objective scale at something less than double the target bonus ensures that balanced attention will be paid to both objectives. Similarly, the even progression of the compounding scale (gross margin) communicates that each incremental basis point in gross margin will add some value to the bonus earned for sales growth.

Put the Brakes on Runaway Earnings. If not carefully tested, compounding relationships harbor a hidden risk of excessive payouts. In the overachievement zone, where both the core and the secondary incentives may accelerate, the compounding effect inherent in conventional linear payout schedules will result in runaway earnings. Figure 8.8 reproduces the performance scales and payout schedules used in Figure 8.7, but in this case the payouts are adjusted and follow a linear progression. The maximum payout under this scenario is 80 percent rather than 60 percent, even though the target payout remains 30 percent. If a more complex compounding structure is used, such as one involving three or four interactive objectives, the need to carefully regulate and test this maximum payout clearly becomes a crucial design consideration.

As mentioned earlier, the payout scheme in Figure 8.7 tempers the compounding effect above target performance, even more than in the windfall zone of the anguine curve, so that overachievement payouts for the secondary objectives are reliant on significant progress toward the core objective. With this structure, the manager's directive emphasizes

Sales Growth		Gross Margin	
Percentage Growth Rate	Bonus % of Base Salary	Gross Margin Percentage	Bonus % of Sales Growth Incentive Earnings
Less than 5%	0%	Less than 25%	0%
6	4	26	10
7	8	27	20
8	12	28	30
9	16	30	40
10	20	32	50
12	24	34	60
14	28	36	70
16	32	38	80
18	36	40	90
20	40	42	100

Figure 8.8 The Risks of a Linear Payout Progression

balanced performance across all objectives in favor of outstanding achievement on even the core objective.

A Payout Grid with Traffic Lights

In this brief digression "back to the future," a timeworn concept—the incentive payout grid—is revisited. Many long-term and some annual incentive plans use a payout grid that blends two dimensions of performance, as illustrated in Figure 8.9. Typically, these grids assign weights to each performance dimension that apply across all ranges of performance. In the example, a 60 percent weight has been assigned to the return objective, and a 40 percent weight is assigned to capital growth. Note that the steps in the grid progress in even increments in each direction, but the steps horizontally are half again as large as the vertical steps. This imbalanced progression creates the 60 percent/40 percent weighting specified for the grid.

With some imaginative refinements, this grid can be converted from a simple payout table to a powerful management communiqué. Looking at the modified grid in Figure 8.10 on a quadrant-by-quadrant basis and recalling the performance zones of the anguine curve, it follows that the payout biases in these quadrants should adhere to the dictates of practical business decisions. Namely, in quadrant I, where both return and growth

Payout Percentage of Target Bonus											
Growth in Invested Capital	Return on Invested Capital										
	8%	9%	10%	11%	12%	13%	14%	15%	16%	17%	18%
Less than 5%	0	12	24	36	48	60	72	84	96	108	120
6%	8					68					128
7	16					76					136
8	24					84					144
9	32					92					152
10	40	52	64	76	88	100	112	124	136	148	160
11	48					108					168
12	56					116					176
13	64					124					184
14	72					132					192
15	80	92	104	116	128	140	152	164	176	188	200

Figure 8.9 Uniformly Weighted Incentive-Payout Grid

Payout Percentage of Target Bonus											
Growth in Invested Capital	Return on Invested Capital										
	8%	9%	10%	11%	12%	13%	14%	15%	16%	17%	18%
Less than 5%	0	10	23	40	57	60	61	64	66	69	70
6%	5					65					81
7	10			I		70		II			93
8	24					84					124
9	38					98					156
10	40	50	63	80	97	100	104	121	138	155	160
11	41					102					162
12	45					119					179
13	49			III		135		IV			195
14	49					138					197
15	50	65	85	110	136	140	144	161	178	195	200

Figure 8.10 Strategically Weighted Incentive-Payout Grid

are below target, it makes good sense to favor the return measure. In quadrant II, where the return on investment is outpacing capital-growth performance, incentive payouts for additional return should decelerate and encourage the manager's aggressive pursuit of opportunities for additional growth.

Analysis of quadrant III reveals a different message. Capital growth is more than satisfactory, but the return has suffered. Thus, the bias in the incentive payouts is abruptly reversed and even more strongly favors incremental return. In quadrant IV, where the manager has exceeded target performance on both dimensions, the grid reverts to its original return bias. (Naturally, this quadrant IV progression should be in lock-step with management's strategy and might just as reasonably favor growth under these conditions.)

In addition to the incentive-weighting scheme just outlined, Figure 8.10 also incorporates the anguine payout pattern throughout the grid. So, as performance approaches the target range for either dimension, the payout progression becomes more gradual. In the windfall and consolation zones, the progression is also very gradual, but in the actuating and excellence zones, the payouts accelerate rapidly.

Engineering without a Blueprint

Used as a reference, the pages in this chapter are likely to become dog-eared before the creaks are worked from the spine of the other chapters. Traditionally, compensation planners designing incentive plans almost always turn first to mechanical devices for the answers to their pay-for-performance questions. These answers appear to be of a purely technical nature and can satisfactorily meet the expectations of a management group that finds comfort in the familiar, current-day compensation-program structures. However, these conventional structures embody almost no challenge to management priorities or preconceptions, and consequently they do little to establish the compensation planner's credibility as a value-added contributor to management policy.

So, a word of caution to the unwary planner who wishes to maintain a low profile: The incentive-engineering topics of this chapter were purposely placed toward the end of the book because they rely heavily on the business-analysis foundation laid in earlier chapters. To use these techniques without being conversant in the company's competitive strategies is a course of even higher risk than the challenge to management priorities that may have been avoided. Beyond the personal risk involved, offering up one of these techniques as an achievement-pay solution without the supporting rationale (that is, why performance measures are assigned specific weights or how the measures interact) is foolhardy and could even convey messages that contradict the business strategy.

9

The Medium and the Message
Equity for the Right Reasons

Throughout this book, the focus has been on annual cash compensation. As we turn now to longer-term reward systems, most of the achievement-pay principles outlined previously also apply. However, the medium of payment—stock or cash—is an added consideration for many public and some private companies (particularly those about to go public) when long-term incentive plans are being designed. Historically, designers of these compensation programs have leaned toward the use of stock, with the underlying assumption that a stock option or other form of stock payment would help to balance a manager's short- and long-term perspectives.

This naive assumption has been fueled by an income-tax structure heavily favoring long-term capital gains. In fact, the bias arising from this favored tax treatment grew to overshadow in many companies the fundamental business purpose of the multiyear incentive plan. With these personal and corporate tax implications clouding the objectives of long-term programs, it is often difficult to discern whether they were primarily intended as capital-accumulation vehicles or as true incentives reinforcing an ownership mind-set. Regardless of the original intent, however, a long-term plan is an *incentive* only if it can be clearly construed as a direct and easily discerned counterbalance to the short-term (annual) incentives. In most cases, though, stock options or grants do not pass this test. So careful evaluation of any stock proposal's merits is a necessary first step in deciding how an equity plan supports a company's compensation objectives.

Now that the 1986 Tax Reform Act has curtailed for individuals almost all of the tax-favored compensation arrangements, companies can more objectively reassess the desirability of stock-based incentive plans. And even if the special capital-gains tax treatment is reinstated, business strategy and motivational intent rather than these tax considerations should be the compensation planner's barometer when gauging the incentive impact of stock programs. Occasionally, conditions within a company may permit a program to simultaneously fulfill both the capital-accumulation and motivational objectives. But, in keeping with the achievement focus of this book, the capital-accumulation purpose will be put aside and the discussion will center on long-term compensation plans as incentives that influence management behavior.

Also, as the distinction is drawn between capital accumulation and long-term incentive programs, the relative value of celebrity CEO stock or stock-option grants in the multimillion-dollar category are not the focal points. Nor is much attention given to the management contracts sporting special stock arrangements that often accompany the current turnaround and leveraged-buyout deals. The emphasis here is on long-term senior- and middle-management incentives aimed exclusively at the counterbalancing objective. Consequently, what is covered in the following pages is a method of addressing this objective with much more conservative amounts of money (or stock) than the megadollars frequently headlined in the business press scorecards.

Specious Reference Points

Compensation policymakers are unfortunately cut adrift in a sea without landmarks when it comes to pinpointing the competitive levels of long-term compensation. Survey data are available that purport to define the annualized values of long-term incentives for companies from varying size and industry categories, relying on value-estimation techniques that at best approximate future stock values based on a host of financial assumptions. Moreover, these surveys may obscure the vast differences in pay practices between the smaller and the very large companies.

Though these differences are highlighted in annual cash-compensation surveys, the effects of company size are far more difficult to measure in the realm of long-term incentives. Survey data are more apt to relate long-term incentive compensation, such as stock-option grants, as a multiple of base salary. For example, an executive earning $100,000 a year in base salary who is reported to have a stock-option multiple of two times has a projected equity value of $200,000 (that is, 10,000 shares optioned at $20 per share). Some more sophisticated surveys attempt to combine all forms of cash and stock long-term payments in a formula that measures the annualized gain an executive can expect (using price/earnings and earnings-per-share projections) as a multiple of base salary. But caution is advised when these more sophisticated data bases are used, since they tend to be biased toward the very large U.S. corporations. And, though difficult to prove with available statistics, it is highly likely that the ratios reported in these surveys grossly overstate the compensation opportunities in smaller and medium-sized corporations.

One recent survey conducted by a leading consultant was surprisingly candid in describing his personal approach to setting long-term incentive-compensation targets. The first step was to forecast the stock price five and ten years into the future based on the company's most optimistic assumptions. Then, the company's executives were polled to determine how much personal capital-accumulation would "make them happy." A simple division of executive "need" by projected gain was used to set long-term incentive payout targets. Although this approach is clearly not scientific, it is probably a more accurate reflection of current practice than any quantitative survey data conveys.

As a starting point, surveys do provide ballpark boundaries for long-term incentive compensation. According to these data, top-tier public companies commonly target annualized long-term payouts at 75 percent to 100 percent of base salary. These percentages decline proportionately with the size of the company and the regression in executive salary levels. Thus, in smaller companies senior executives may have an annualized opportunity of only 15 percent to 50 percent of base salary derived from their long-term incentive plans. Acknowledging the breadth of these ranges, the compensation planner must look beyond these data for definitive guidance on *who* participates in these incentives and at *what opportunity level*. To get these answers, the planner should rely on introspection (rather than external data bases) to decide what makes sense for a specific position and how the program fits a company's size and financial welfare.

More than for any other component of compensation, long-term incentive participation has been arbitrarily determined and, as a result, postured more as a recognition device than as a true incentive. Though most companies will tout a "strategic impact" criterion for the participation of any given executive, few consistently put this rationale to the acid test. To step outside this rhetoric, the reader should return to the compensation risk equation illustrated in Figure 5.2 and review the equation's criteria, keeping an eye out for their special meaning as indicators of management's leverage on the long-term welfare of a business. In a vein similar to this earlier discussion, long-term (or strategic) leverage comes from two sources: the external dynamics of a business and the personal impact imputed to a manager based on the organization and decision processes of the company.

Referencing the environmental (or external) factors—market and technological stability, growth objectives, and competitive position—used in chapter 5 to define annual pay risk (see Figure 5.3), conclusions about long-term pay risk follow much the same logic. Namely, in more volatile marketing and technological climates, long-term commitments and visionary planning are crucial to safeguarding a company's market position and stimulating the innovation necessary to preserve its competitive stature. Likewise, high growth objectives and niche marketing call for aggressive and tenacious managerial guidance that protects footholds with key customers while constantly searching for growth opportunities created by competitors' weaknesses.

Turning to the individual position criteria for pay risk, though, the logic set forth for determining annual risk amounts must be modified to provide useful insights on long-term incentive policy. First, only three of the criteria shown in Figures 5.5 and 5.6 apply to this discussion of long-term incentives (namely, execution proximity, independence of action, and consequence of action). In considering long-term incentives, execution proximity must reflect the *influence* of a position on strategic decisions (that is, their membership in the policy inner sanctum) rather than its accountability for tactical execution of a strategy. Positions with this proximity, if they can also exercise considerable independence in committing company resources to a long-term course of action, would normally participate at the top of the long-term incentive scale. Thus, for all three of these criteria, a strategic context is the basis for measuring position impact.

A reconstituted version of the position risk profile is shown in Figure 9.1 and identifies three categories of positions for setting long-term compensation policy. These categories are then used to assign a position to a long-term risk level according to the following guidelines:

Long-Term Risk Classification	Annualized Long-Term Risk (Multiple of Target Annual Bonus)
Policymaker	1.0X–2.0X
Policy planner	0.5X–0.75X
Nonparticipants	0

As in the earlier evaluation of annual risk policy, one may interpret these ranges by matching the top end of each bracket to companies scoring

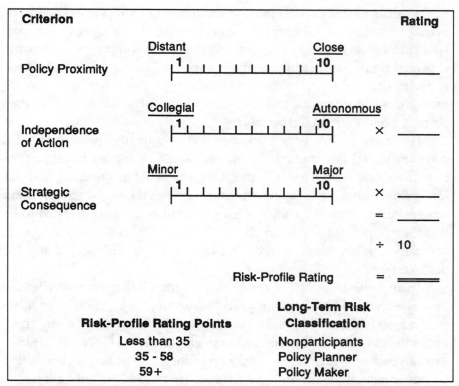

Figure 9.1 Evaluating a Position for Long-Term Incentives

high on the environmental criteria, and vice versa for those on the lower end of this scale.

The somewhat unusual expression of these targets as a multiple of annual bonus targets reinforces the risk equity premise set forth in chapter 5. To paraphrase this premise, the assignment of compensation risk targets should not be artificially constrained by base-salary hierarchies but rather should coincide with the characteristics of each individual position. Following this philosophy and calculating long-term risk targets as a multiple of the annual bonus rather than of the base salary precludes positions with high base salaries from automatically having the greatest amount of pay at risk. Above all, this system for setting long-term incentive policy achieves a natural counterbalance between annual and long-term priorities by guaranteeing the alignment of short- and long-term incentive amounts.

Equity or Not Equity

At first glance, stock ownership is credited with all of the desired attributes of a long-term incentive. Its direct linkage to changes in company (and stockholder) value and its imputed ties to the company's current and expected future performance make it a natural favorite of compensation planners and executives alike. Layer on top of these attributes the advantageous corporate-tax and cash-flow effects of stock, and this viewpoint is even more understandable.

There are no industry standards that specify the proportion of a company's total outstanding shares that should be owned by executives to incite them to do what is best for the shareholder. But most business leaders and commentators purport that executives should own a significant amount of stock and that their relatively small holdings (estimated to be less than 1 percent for 90 percent of the CEOs of the top 250 U.S. companies) is the single biggest reason for the weak state of pay for performance.

To alter this trend, some companies are installing "mandatory" stock purchase plans. (This use of the word "mandatory" is certainly a candidate for "nospeak," since it usually is defined as "to encourage or to urge" rather than to "require" as a condition of employment.) Under these plans, executives are "urged" to use a portion of their annual bonus distribution to buy common stock, and they are "encouraged" to hold the stock throughout their employment with the company.

Consistent with the spirit of this book, though, we will once again take a half-step backward to pose a more basic question: What long-term incentive structures best fit a company's business and its leadership style? Several primary techniques for putting stock in the hands of employees have evolved over the past 30 years. But to place these techniques in their proper context within the full range of long-term incentive alternatives, a brief review of the menu is offered as a handy synopsis of the more extensive appendix B, and then a policy-development model is discussed to assist the compensation planner in selecting the most appropriate incentive program.

The Long-Term Incentive Policy Menu

The range of alternative long-term compensation programs can be grouped into four broad categories, with variations in each category. These groupings are based primarily on how closely the plans link long-term rewards to *internal* unit or company financial-performance measures or to *external* market performance. The four categories are as follows:

▌ **Stock Ownership Plans**
Incentive stock options (ISO)
Nonqualified stock options (NQSO)
Restricted stock
Book-value stock purchase
▌ **Shadow Stock Ownership Plans**
Stock appreciation rights (SAR)
Phantom stock
Dividend equivalents
▌ **Strategic Performance Plans**
Performance units
Consistency multipliers
Simulated equity
Intrinsic market value (IMV)
Economic value added (EVA)
▌ **Hybrid Plans**
Performance unit/option
ISO/SAR
Performance shares

Stock Ownership Plans. In these plans an executive is granted either a conditioned right to shares or an option to purchase shares in the future at a favorable price (or, as a recent innovation, at a premium price). With restricted stock, a wide range of qualifying conditions can limit the access to the shares granted, including conditions related to specific long-range performance or length of service. But, more typically, the restricted stock plan's linkage to company performance is only implicit, and the primary emphasis is on external market-value increases. On the other hand, the book-value stock-purchase arrangement is as its name implies—dependent on book- rather than market-value increases—thereby insulating the compensation program from the potential vagaries of the market.

Shadow Stock Ownership Plans. Each of the plans in this category is directly linked to stock performance—either dividend payouts or stock price appreciation. Registered shares are not owned by the executive, nor is the executive required to make any investment. Traditionally, stock appreciation rights (SARs) have been used in tandem with stock options to fund the stock purchase. Phantom stock and dividend equivalents are also used to mirror a specific aspect of shareholder value and pay rewards consistent with the increase in that value.

Strategic Performance Plans. Unlike the stock-based plans outlined above, strategic performance plans use internal performance measures to focus management's attention on long-term objectives. In this manner, the company can explicitly define and reward for its own performance priorities independent of the market pricing mechanism. The performance unit and consistency multiplier concepts make no attempt to track directly the underlying determinants of a company's value, whereas the other concepts listed try to simulate market value or rely on accounting formulas to estimate that value. Payouts for these strategic performance plans are typically made in cash, but a company's stock can also be used.

Hybrid Plans. At this point it is probably evident that there are numerous ways to mix and match the various types of plans to meet unique compensation objectives. The plans included in this category represent only a small sample of the potential combinations that can be used. Typically, these combinations mix two of the above programs to achieve a balance between internal strategic performance and the market's evaluation of a company's progress. (The ISO/SAR combination is an exception to this rule in that it is based only on the market's evaluation of a stock.)

Selecting from the Policy Menu

Business analysis has been the prevailing theme of this book, guiding the planner's choice of a salary hierarchy, the determination of compensation mix, the selection and weighting of performance measures, and now, the preference for cash or stock as a medium for long-term incentives. In making this final compensation-policy decision, the compensation planner must draw on many of the previous discussions in order to qualitatively assess which of the items on the policy menu will deliver the strongest and clearest message to the manager. To predict the actual impact of a stock program on executive behavior, though, the compensation planner must shift the focus from familiar platitudes and analyze how the program will fit the company's ownership structure, leadership style, and management practices. As the basis of this evaluation, the four independent traits summarized in Figure 9.2 are used to characterize the managerial environment.

Strategy Cell. In chapter 7, the business portfolio lattice was used to separate business units into four categories depending on their competitive strategy: lions, wildcats, cows, and dogs. Once again, these classes are useful in guiding the compensation planner to a long-term compensation policy that supports the business mission. In a wildcat business,

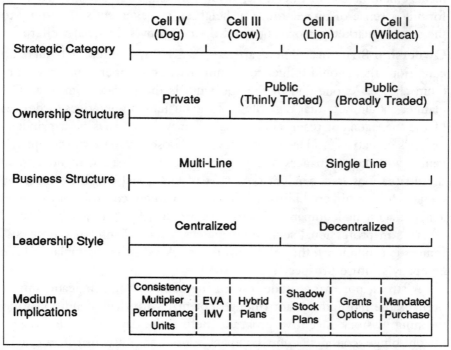

Figure 9.2 Evaluating Long-Term Incentive Medium Alternatives

long-term gain is the most prominent focus as the business strives to achieve commercial viability and financial credibility. Stock purchase is desirable for this type of business, particularly in the context of an initial public offering, since equity buy-in may be the most effective and affordable means to attract managerial talent. (Executive loans or a program of paced investments are often used to finance the executives' stock purchase.) As a business moves out of this stage of development into the established lion category, the value of stock is more clearly defined and should be attractive as an investment to the senior- and middle-management groups. Thus, restricted stock grants, stock options, and stock purchase programs are all potentially useful long-term incentives for businesses in this category.

Moving into cells III and IV, it is likely that the internal management structure of a company will become more rigid and bureaucratic and that the stock value is more closely tied to swings in the total market (or a particular industry's cycles) rather than to the company's independent performance. Under these conditions, stock ownership is a weaker incentive, and cash tied to internal value measures has a greater impact on management behavior. In cell III, shadow stock, while not strongly reinforcing a sense of ownership, can heighten management's sensitivity to the stock's market performance and the company's financial welfare.

Ownership Structure. There are essentially three different ownership conditions that should influence a compensation planner's incentive-medium choice. At one end of the spectrum is the private company. The planner should note that regardless of the business imperatives or desires of the management team, equity sharing may not always be a principal owner's objective. And even if the owner chooses to share the company's equity with key managers, the incentive impact of stock ownership in these situations is dependent on a host of emotional considerations: the owner's leadership credibility; the locus of customer control (for example, a manufacturing company's customers are usually "company-owned," whereas in professional service businesses, personal influence over customers is prominent); the validity of the stock valuation formula; and the company's future prospects.

A strong positive attitude toward the company and its leadership is perhaps the most important (though not mandatory) precondition for a meaningful stock-incentive program. Before the days of the leveraged-buyout binge, confidence in a company's leadership was usually a crucial prerequisite to one's investment in that company's stock. Some companies have fallen into the trap of reversing the cart and the horse by introducing stock as a means of building cohesion and creating an emotional "buy-in" to a company's leadership and direction. However, if there is no preexisting foundation of confidence in the company's leadership, it is unlikely that substituting stock for spendable, taxable cash will alter the manager's ownership mind-set. Nonetheless, even without this foundation the remaining factors may override this void and support the use of stock. If there are strong personal ties to key customers, and if the management team views the valuation formula and future prospects of the company in a positive light, stock ownership should still be considered, but only with a buy-in provision that transforms the manager from simply an employee to a stakeholder who shares the principal owner's risks and vision.

Public companies with thinly traded stock have a particularly difficult task in using stock-based incentives, since managers inside these companies often believe that stock price is more sensitive to the trading volume in the narrow market of the actively traded shares than it is to company performance. Consequently, the perception of a clear linkage between performance and stock value is not easily created in these situations, and it is relevant to question whether managers believe that their actions and strategies will truly be reflected in the stock value and will not be undermined by the whims of the principal owner(s). The book-value stock-purchase arrangement may be a preferable long-term incentive vehicle for these closely held companies, because executive gains are dependent on book- rather than market-value increases.

Broadly traded public companies present no obstacles in terms of the market valuation process. Nonetheless, to determine the potential incentive value of stock for these companies the compensation planner should not be influenced by the convenient availability of this payout medium but rather by the strategy analysis just discussed and the two traits yet to be examined.

Business Structure. Stock-ownership plans are most applicable when the company is in a single line of business and is organized functionally. In these cases, managers clearly identify their own contributions to the total company's results and readily perceive their impact on the stock value. A homogeneous business structure, however, is not necessarily the final word on the use of stock. An anecdote related by a consulting colleague illustrates an attitude that, though prevalent, is certainly counter to the spirit of this book. If seems that our colleague was making a call with a senior partner of her firm on a company made up of several silver mining operations. The partner was eager to sell the CEO of this company on the idea of an incentive stock option plan. In conversation, our colleague asked the CEO what he thought was the single most important factor influencing the company's stock price. Without hesitation he answered, "The price of silver." Our colleague quickly pointed out that, since the Hunt brothers did not work for this company, it would probably be better to base the company's long-term incentive on something over which the executives had greater control. Even though this was indisputably good advice, the senior partner was incredulous at this lapse in salesmanship.

The connection between results and stock value is even further diluted as a company diversifies its portfolio of businesses. So in companies made up of diverse and autonomous divisions, cash tied to a division's own performance rather than stock is usually a preferable form of short- *and* long-term incentive compensation (except perhaps for the most-senior management positions). And in this light, strategic performance plans are often the most useful in rewarding for the individual contributions to company value that a separate business unit makes. But although these types of plans provide considerable flexibility, they also require a degree of planning and financial sophistication not found in many companies. Therefore, the policy planner should move cautiously in this direction to assure that the incentive design is not outpacing the company's planning and performance-management systems.

Leadership Style. A highly centralized or autocratic decision-making environment dictates that if stock is used at all, participation must be limited to the select few decision makers. Under these conditions, the compensation planner should not succumb to the popular delusion that placing stock (or options) in the hands of a broader group of managers will somehow result in a spirit of teamwork and participative management. Rather, the planner may have to consider additional annual incentive opportunities for these disenfranchised managers in order to maintain a competitive total-compensation package and to avoid the fallacious inclusion of these managers in a long-term stock incentive.

Possibly the most difficult challenge for the compensation planner in assessing this leadership-style trait is determining the policy implications for companies that lie somewhere between the extremes of centralization and decentralization. In this middle ground, hybrid plans that combine cash and stock may be the best fit. But again, participation must be carefully tailored to the company's decision-making network and guided by the strategy category and business-line homogeneity traits.

Stock Status

The prescriptions for long-term incentive-medium policy are not exact, and they require a high degree of judgment and interpretation. Using any trait singularly will almost always lead to the wrong conclusion, and, where stock ownership is involved, it runs the risk of casting the entire long-term program in a trivial and penurious light. For example, a publishing company with one of the leading national magazines among its properties has its stock traded publicly, but its ownership is heavily concentrated in a single family. The strategy cell of this company in its growth/turnaround mode would clearly argue for the use of stock as a senior-management incentive. However, the executive group lacks confidence in the principal owner's leadership, the stock has a history of unexplained price gyrations in the market, and the leadership style is highly centralized. A stock program in this environment, even if couched as restricted grants, could easily be interpreted as a paltry substitute for cash. So the policy planner's analysis of long-term incentive media is similar to all that has preceded it. Shortcuts cannot be taken, and the compensation planner must have in-depth knowledge of a company's management processes and a thorough understanding of its competitve posture to enable thoughtful application of the foregoing principles in formulating a compensation policy.

A primary aim throughout this book has been to encourage the compensation planner to venture out of the shadows of conventional practice and to examine new ways of uniting compensation policy with the unique characteristics of a business. This section on long-term compensation is no exception as it leads the planner into a wilderness of incentive-pay dogma that is virtually uncharted. But each time new questions are asked or old "truths" are challenged with business logic, incentive compensation inches closer to becoming a viable management system that is instrumental to strategy execution.

=== 10 ===
Postscript

Designing a compensation program that will act as a personal incentive for employees to improve their achievement levels is not a study in gimmickry; rather, it requires hard work and diligent communication. In each chapter of this book we have taken well-aimed shots to the midsection of copycat policy formulation; and we have attempted to demonstrate the futility of management's search for the "One-Minute, Theory XYZ, Quick, Pay-for-Performance" fix. Professional management lore has become a limitless reservoir of these "simple truths" that claim to cure all maladies, and consequently any achievement-pay program colored by even the slightest tint of complexity stands a good chance of being summarily rejected.

But what is management's track record over the years in its application of these "simple truths"? A closer examination of the checkered past reveals that "truth" has the approximate half-life of any given hem length, and that insight and old-fashioned know-how are the timeless and incorruptible beacons for formulating sound management policy.

Blatant examples of misalignment between compensation and management performance have generated much press in recent years. Perhaps the most notable of these incidents was the now-infamous executive bonus payments made to General Motors executives while the company was losing money and demanding give-backs from the unions. One generic prescription for this misalignment has been "pay-for-performance" programs that share a company's fortunes (and misfortunes) broadly with the work force. However, if one considers the intricacy of the issues outlined in the foregoing pages, these simple pay-for-performance prescriptions are lacking the uncommon degree of common sense required to create competitive advantage.

Without question, achievement pay is an extremely complex and difficult concept to implement successfully. It demands thoughtful business analysis to properly fit compensation strategy to the values and personality of a particular company. Management must make reasoned decisions about pay strategies that diverge from market pay practices, and about the positions that should be impacted by these divergent strategies. Moreover, compensation hierarchies must be built with salary progressions and ranges that are in tune with the individual character and mission of each functional or business unit. Finally, incentive strategies must carefully match high-risk compensation arrangements to functions or positions emphasizing individual initiative, and more modest levels of compensation risk to functions placing a premium on teamwork and familial employee relationships.

Few companies commit the necessary resources when they embark on an achievement-pay campaign, and responsibility for its execution is usually delegated to human resources professionals (either inside or outside the company). But these professionals rarely include a business analyst within their ranks. The achievement-pay product therefore becomes a superstructure of technically and mechanically sound components built on a crumbling foundation of competitive compensation practices and misconstrued notions of internal equity. Furthermore, as these programs are designed, line managers' intuitive specifications either have been ignored or have gone unchallenged—two sins of equal severity.

To escape these pitfalls, a framework for relating each element of compensation strategy to the performance management imperatives is mandatory. If such a framework is used, generic concepts will be either rejected out of hand or subjected to stringent tests of their applicability. Above all, compensation policymakers will have a firm rationale to tailor compensation policy to the changes in the business environment and organization as they occur and will take their rightful seat alongside the CEO as valued counselors on business strategy.

= Appendix A =

Executive Pay Takes a Random Walk

Analysis of the *Business Week* Scoreboard

The *Business Week* Scoreboard examines the relationship between pay and performance in two ways: It compares an executive's salary with the company's total return to shareholders, defined as stock appreciation plus dividends over a three-year period; a second comparison measures pay versus corporate profitability for the same three-year period. In addition, the *Scoreboard* analysis ranks the pay-for-performance efficiency of companies within an industry group, but it carefully avoids drawing any global conclusions spanning the entire data base. So, to validate the connection between pay and performance on a wider scale, it is necessary to take the analysis one step further.

It is a well-accepted premise that company size has a substantial impact on executive pay levels, so in the first step of reorganizing the data, this was filtered out of the *Business Week* statistics before any cross-industry (or even intra-industry) analysis was done. This filtering process was accomplished in two stages. First, a single-regression equation fitting pay to company size was developed to measure the gap between actual pay levels and predicted pay based solely on sales size. Then this gap was plotted against the two key measures of performance (Figures A.1 and A.2)—average annual return on equity and average annual stock value appreciation—to assess how these performance variables might further explain the variation in pay levels. For purposes of this analysis, a total period of five years (based on three successive surveys) was used to smooth the effects of industry cycles and other data anomalies.

The scattergrams clearly paint a picutre of the randomness of the pay-for-performance connection. Though one would expect a pattern of data points along a northeasterly diagonal, the points acually exhibit no discernible pattern and in fact offer stark contradictions. In Figure A.1, for example, two companies with a 40 percent average return on equity paid their executives vastly differing amounts of money over the past five years—one exceeding the compensation level predicted by sales size by about $4 million a year and the other falling short by about $500,000 a year. Turning to Figure A.2, two other companies that paid their executives at exactly the same level predicted by the sales regression had widely varying levels of stock appreciation in the five-year period (that is, 3 percent vs. 38 percent).

Figure A.3 further demonstrates the chasm between pay and company achievements. By segmenting the data base into four quartiles of perfor-

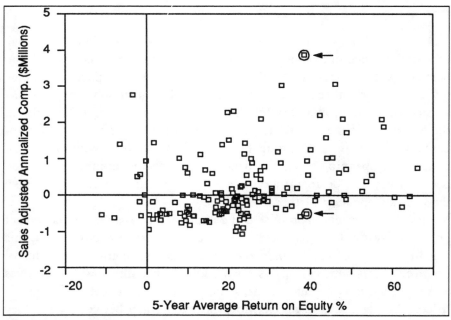

Figure A.1 Compensation versus Return on Equity

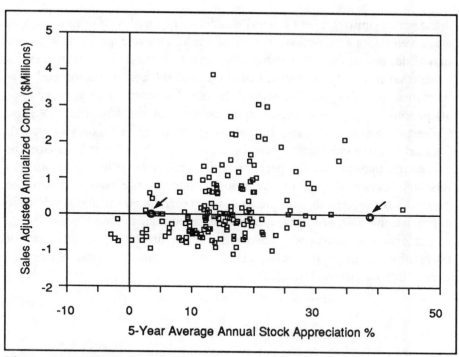

Figure A.2 Compensation versus Stock Appreciation

Percent of Total Observations (n = 163)				
ROE Quartile	Compensation Quartile			
	I	*II*	*III*	*IV*
I	**11%**	9%	4%	1%
II	5	**8**	8	5
III	5	6	**9**	6
IV	4	4	4	**13**
Stock Appreciation Quartile	*I*	*II*	*III*	*IV*
I	**12%**	7%	4%	4%
II	7	**5**	7	9
III	5	7	**7**	10
IV	2	6	6	**17**

Figure A.3 Comparison of Compensation and Performance Quartiles mance and, similarly, into four sales-adjusted quartiles of compensation, we developed a cross-classification of these data that provides a crude, first-order test of the relationships. Nonetheless, the disappointing results reveal that in nearly 60 percent of the cases, the compensation and performance quartiles are mismatched. In fact, for stock value appreciation, 30 percent of the cases are at opposite ends of the spectrum (i.e., the highest-paid executives are the lowest-performing ones, or vice versa). Similarly, when company return-on-equity performance is compared to pay, nearly one-quarter (23 percent) of the observations lie in the extreme misclassification sectors of the grid. Although only two performance measures are used in this simple analysis (return on equity and stock value appreciation), and, arguably, multivariate techniques using a wider range of performance measures might yield a better fit, the visible evidence of correlation in these pay relationships that investors should reasonably expect is nonexistent.

= Appendix B =

A Précis of Long-Term Reward Systems

CONTENTS
I. Stock Ownership Plans
Incentive stock options (ISO)
Nonqualified stock options (NQSO)
Restricted stock
Book-value stock purchase

II. Shadow Stock Ownership Plans
Stock appreciation rights (SAR)
Phantom stock
Dividend equivalents

III. Strategic Performance Plans
Performance units
Simulated equity
Intrinsic market value (IMV)
Economic value added (EVA)
Consistency multiplier

IV. Hybrid Plans
Performance unit/option
Performance shares

I. Stock Ownership Plans

Incentive Stock Options (ISO)

Description: Option to purchase shares of company stock at 100% of fair market value on date of grant for a period of up to ten years. Must be designed to meet statutory limits on the aggregate fair market value of stock exercisable in a given year.

Tax Treatment—Executive: At exercise there is no tax. Upon sale of stock, the gain is taxed as ordinary income.

Tax Treatment—Company: No tax deduction at time of exercise.

Accounting Treatment: No expense recognizable. Dilution may occur since options are common stock equivalents. Option proceeds are credited to paid-in capital.

Insider Trading Considerations: *Grant* of option will not be considered a "purchase" if the plan meets certain requirements relating to administration by disinterested parties, shareholder approval, limits on benefits, and nontransferability of the option.

Exercise of options will be considered a "purchase" and will be matched with any "sale" in the preceding or following six months.

Qualifications:

- Three-month exercise limitation on termination, including retirement
- Maximum exercisable amount in one year is $100,000 (based on ISO grant price)
- Cannot be granted to executive owning more than 10% of voting stock unless option granted at 110% of market value

Nonqualified Stock Options (NQSO)

Description: Option to purchase shares of company stock at a stated price over a period of time, frequently ten years. Option price equal to 100% of market value on date of grant (or may be issued at a premium striking price). Options are sometimes discounted and this will affect tax and accounting treatment.

Tax Treatment—Executive: At exercise the excess of the fair market value of the stock over the option price is taxed as ordinary income and is subject to withholding. Taxation for insiders may be delayed upon exercise to the end of the required six-month holding period. Any discount of the option price from fair market value is taxable at time of *grant*.

Tax Treatment—Company: Tax deduction in the amount of the executive's income from the option at the same time the executive is taxed. Any discount of the option price is deductible at time of grant.

Accounting Treatment: No expense recognizable if both the number and price of optioned shares are fixed at the date of grant. Dilution may occur, however, since options are common stock equivalents. The option proceeds savings are credited to paid-in capital.

Insider Trading Considerations: Same as those cited under Incentive Stock Options.

Restricted Stock

Description: An award of stock that is nontransferable and/or subject to a substantial risk of forfeiture. These restrictions lapse over a period of years. Dividends are paid to executives as declared. If plan involves the sale of stock, the executive's purchase price may be substantially below the fair market value. This will affect tax and accounting treatment. Restrictions may include specific financial performance criteria.

Tax Treatment—Executive:
- *Timing*: Executive may elect to pay tax at date of award. If this timing is not elected, a tax liability arises when stock is transferable or is no longer subject to substantial risk of forfeiture, whichever is earlier.
- *Amount*: The excess of the value of the stock over the price at date of award is taxed as ordinary income and is subject to withholding. If an award-date taxation is elected, the value is determined without regard to any restrictions other than a restriction that has an indefinite term.

■ *Dividends*: Dividends are treated as compensation income while restrictions are in force, unless executive elects to be taxed currently.

■ *Note*: If executive elects to be taxed at the time of award and subsequently forfeits the stock, there is no recovery of taxes.

Tax Treatment—Company: On date executive is taxed, tax deduction in the amount of the executive's income is permissible. The deduction will be denied if the company fails to withhold.

Accounting Treatment: The value of the stock at the time of award is charged as a compensation expense over the period for which the related service is performed (usually the restriction period). Interperiod tax allocation may be required if the company's tax deduction on the "spread" at the grant date occurs in a later period than when the accounting expense is charged. Any tax savings on postgrant appreciation bypasses the income statement and is posted directly to the additional paid-in capital account on the balance sheet.

Insider Trading Considerations: Grant will not be considered a "purchase" if the plan meets certain requirements related to administration by disinterested parties, shareholder limits on benefits, and if the participant has no control over the timing of share receipts.

Qualifications—Company: If stock appreciates after award date, actual tax deduction will be greater than amount taken for book income.

Book-Value Stock Purchase

Description: Executive is offered opportunities to purchase stock whose price is determined by reference to book value. Offer is usually for a limited time. Shares must be resold to the company at a later date at the current–per-share book value. Shares for a book-value plan may be a separate, nonvoting class of stock. Holders of this class of stock could receive dividends as paid. Book value may be used in lieu of market value in the design of stock options, stock appreciation rights, and phantom stock plans. Shares granted at a discount will affect tax and accounting treatment.

Tax Treatment—Executive:
- At purchase, no tax consequences.
- At sale, increase in book value from date of purchase is taxed as ordinary income.
- Dividends are taxed at ordinary income rates when received.

Tax Treatment—Company: At purchase, resale, or payment of dividends, company gets no tax deduction.

Accounting Treatment: No expense is recognizable. Amounts received from executives for purchases are credited to paid-in capital.

Insider Trading Considerations: Same as those cited under ISOs.

Qualifications: Could lead to retention of low earning assets and avoidance of risk investments.

II. Shadow Stock Ownership Plans

Stock Appreciation Rights (SAR)

Description: Rights normally granted in tandem with an option where the executive, *in lieu of exercising the option*, can receive a payment equal to the difference between the option price and the current market value of the stock. SARs may be attached to ISOs if IRS requirements concerning exercise are met. SARs may also be granted on a "stand-alone" basis without an option. Payment of rights may be in cash, stock, or combination.

Tax Treatment—Executive: On exercise of right, value of right is taxed as ordinary income and is subject to withholding.

Tax Treatment—Company: On exercise date, tax deduction in the amount of the executive's income is permissible.

Accounting Treatment: The assumption in most instances is that the SAR, not the stock option, will be exercised. As such, the value of the right, i.e., the excess of the market value of the stock over the option price (at the close of each accounting period), is a compensation expense that is accrued over the period the SAR is outstanding. Interperiod tax allocation may be required if the company's tax deduction occurs in a later period than the accounting expense is charged.

Insider Trading Considerations:
- Grant of a right will not be considered a "purchase" if the plan meets certain requirements relating to administration by disinterested parties, shareholder approval, limits on benefits, and nontransferability of the option and related right.
- Any payment of the SAR in cash is not a "purchase" and/or "sale" if: the company files certain financial data with the SEC; the plan requires a six-month holding period; is administered by disinterested parties; has shareholder approval; and permits exercise only during a "window period" (third through twelfth business day period following the release of quarterly or annual company financial statements).

Qualifications—Executive:
- Possibility of large gains may be limited by maximums imposed to limit accounting charge.
- Any exercise for cash by insiders must be made in a short period after quarterly financial statements are released. This timing may not produce the optimum gain.
- If SARs are granted independent of options, the executive may be taxed on the increase in SAR value if the SAR expires unexercised at the end of its term.

Phantom Stock

Description: Units analogous to company shares are granted to executives. The value of the units equals the appreciation in the market value of the stock underlying the units. Phantom units are valued at a fixed date. Typically, the valuation is at retirement, or five to fifteen years after the grant. Actual payment may be in cash or stock or both. Dividend equivalents may be accrued.

Tax/Accounting/Insider Trading Considerations: Phantom stock mirrors SAR tax, accounting, and insider trading treatment.

Dividend Equivalents

Description: Units analogous to company shares are granted to executives. Dividends paid on common shares are credited to dividend equivalent units and paid out in cash or actual common stock.

Tax/Accounting Treatment: Dividend equivalent units mirror the SAR tax and accounting treatment.

III. Strategic Performance Plans

Performance Units

Description: Executive is contingently awarded units at the beginning of a performance cycle, each of which is assigned an arbitrary dollar value. The number of the units at the end of the cycle depends on the extent to which financial objectives have been achieved. (Alternatively, the number of the units might be fixed with the value of units varying with performance.) The duration of the performance cycle varies by company but is typically three to five years. Financial objectives may relate to such items as cumulative growth in EPS or improvement in ROI. Actual payment may be in cash and/or stock.

Tax Treatment—Executive: On payment date value of the award paid is taxed as ordinary income and is subject to withholding.

Tax Treatment—Company: On payment date, tax deduction in the amount of the executive's income is permissible.

Accounting Treatment: The value of the units is a compensation expense that is estimated and accrued over the period during which related services are performed. Interperiod tax allocation may be required if the company's tax deduction occurs in a later period than the accounting expense is charged.

Insider Trading Considerations: Full or partial stock payment will not be considered a "purchase" and/or "sale" if the plan meets certain requirements relating to administration by disinterested parties, shareholder approval, limits on benefits, and if the executive has no control over the timing or form of share receipts.

Simulated Equity

Description: Units with an arbitrary value are granted to the executive at the beginning of the plan cycle. The value of the units increases annually based on one or more financial performance criteria. At the end of the plan cycle, the executive receives the appreciated value of the units (in cash or stock). During the plan cycle, "dividends" are paid based on the *current* value of the units *and* based on the achievement of annual strategic milestones.

Tax/Accounting/Insider Trading Considerations: Same as for performance units.

Intrinsic Market Value

Description: Units with an arbitrary value are granted to the executive at the beginning of the plan cycle. A *total return index* is established based on adding the ROI and book-value growth of the measured business unit. The value of the executive's units is then determined by how much the index value exceeds or falls short of the firm's cost of capital. In this way, the plan is intended to simulate for an imbedded division or business unit the market-to-book value-pricing mechanism of a publicly traded issue.

Tax/Accounting/Insider Trading Consideration: Same as for performance units.

Economic Value Added

Description: A financial model, developed by Stern Stewart & Company, measures annual increments in the intrinsic value of a company with the following formula:

$$EVA = (R - C) \times Capital$$

In this model, R is the rate of return on invested capital, and C is the cost of capital (approximated using a risk-premium approach to the firm's actual cost of equity capital and a weighted average of the equity and debt capital costs).

This methodology, according to Stern Stewart, creates four important long-term incentives for managers:

∎ To improve profits derived from existing businesses

- To invest capital for growth, but only where the return exceeds the cost of capital
- To halt investment in operations returning less than the cost of capital
- To withdraw capital from uneconomic activities

Incentive plans tied to EVA can be structured along the traditional lines of earnings-based annual programs with targets set for EVA instead of net income. However, EVA is probably an even more effective incentive over an extended period in which a "bank" of value-added dollars is accumulated and shared by key executives in much the same manner as they might be in stock appreciation.

Tax/Accounting/Insider Trading Considerations: Same as for performance units.

Consistency Multiplier

Description: A simple method of rewarding managers for consistent performance over an extended period. A threshold of performance, usually expressed as a *percentage* of the *annual* target bonus, is established as the qualifying hurdle for this long-term incentive. Then a bonus premium or multiplier is paid based on the number of years a manager's performance qualifies. This premium is usually expressed as a percentage of the *cumulative incentive* earnings for the qualifying years. Thus, if a three-year period is designated as the long-term performance cycle, the consistency multiplier might be defined so that if two out of three years qualify, a 20% premium would be paid (i.e., 20% of the cumulative incentive earnings for two qualifying years); and if all three years qualify, a 40% premium would be paid on the cumulative incentive earnings for all three qualifying years.

Tax/Accounting/Insider Trading Considerations: Same as for performance units.

IV. Hybrid Plans

Performance Unit/Options

Description: The simultaneous grant of performance units and a non-qualified option (granted at market value). Payout from units may be in *cash* to enable executives to pay taxes on option exercise or to help finance the exercise. Some programs provide for cancellation of one award when gain is realized from the other award; such cancellations are not permissible in conjunction with an ISO. Options granted at a discount will affect tax and accounting treatment.

Tax Treatment—Executive:
- On payment of units' value, award is taxed as ordinary income and is subject to withholding.
- On exercise of option, the excess of the market value of the stock over the option price is taxed as ordinary income and is subject to withholding.

Tax Treatment—Company:
- On payment of units' value, tax deduction in the amount of the executive's income is permissible.
- On exercise of option, tax deduction in the amount of the executive's income at the same time executive is taxed is permissible.

Accounting Treatment: Each part of the plan is accounted for separately, ignoring the existence of the other part. The accounting treatment is consistent with the provisions described for each component part.

Insider Trading Considerations: Same as for component parts of the plan.

Performance Shares

Description: Executive is contingently awarded a fixed number of common shares at the beginning of a performance cycle. The number of shares payable at the end of the cycle depends on the extent to which financial objectives have been achieved. The value received by the executive depends both on the number of shares earned and their market value at the time of payment.

Duration of the performance cycle varies but is typically three to five years. Financial objectives are typically based on cumulative growth in EPS or improvement in ROI.

Tax Treatment—Executive: On payment date, value of award is taxed as ordinary income and is subject to withholding.

Tax Treatment—Company: On payment date, tax deduction equal to the amount of the executive's income is permissible.

Accounting Treatment: The value of the shares is a compensation expense that is estimated and accrued over the period during which related services are performed. Unlike a performance-unit plan, changes in the market value of the stock are also reflected. Interperiod tax allocation may be required if the company's tax deduction occurs in a later period than the accounting expense is charged.

Insider Trading Considerations:

■ Award of performance shares will not be considered a "purchase" if the plan meets certain requirements relating to administration by disinterested parties, shareholder approval, and limits on benefits.

■ Full or partial cash or stock payment will not be considered a "purchase" and/or "sale" if the above conditions are met and if the executive has no control over the timing or form of receipt.

References

Periodicals

"Executive Compensation Scoreboard." *Business Week*, May 4, 1987, 58–94.

"Executive Compensation Scoreboard." *Business Week*, May 2, 1988, 57–91.

"Executive Compensation Scoreboard." *Business Week*, May 1, 1989, 53–83.

Fierman, Jaclyn. "The People Who Set the CEO's Pay." *Fortune*, March 12, 1990, 58–66.

Books

Crystal, Graef S. *Executive Compensation*. New York: Amacom, 1978.

Galbraith, Jay R., and Nathanson, Daniel A. *Strategy Implementation: The Role of Structure and Process*. St. Paul, MN: West Publishing Co., 1978.

Hofer, Charles W., and Schendel, Dan. *Strategy Formulation: Analytical Concepts*. St. Paul, MN: West Publishing Co., 1978.

Peters, Thomas J., and Waterman, Robert H. Jr. *In Search of Excellence* New York: Harper & Row, 1982.

Porter, Michael E. *Competitive Strategy*. New York: The Free Press, 1980.

Smith, Adam. *Paper Money*. New York: Summit Books, 1981.

Index

A

Ameritech 79
Ashland Oil 127
At-risk pay 28–9, 42–3, 59, 65,
    73, 100–02
    at-risk pay (defined) 42–3
    communication of 60–1
    composite risk profile (com-
        pany) 106–9
    composite risk profile (posi-
        tion) 112–5
    evaluation models 106–17
    fitness for 106
    job security 105, 165
leveraged compensation system
    60, 65
    low risk cultures 106, 109
    purposes of 103–4

B

Ben & Jerry's 23
Board compensation committees
    12, 22, 146
Boeing Co. 127
Boston Consulting Group 85,
    151
Business strategy
    business unit level 133
    competitive advantage 1, 34,
        132–3, 151
    competitive strategy 6–8, 11,
        24–5, 33, 197
    corporate level 132–3
    distinctive competencies
        132–3
    functional area 132–3, 139,
        148
    resource deployment 132
    scope 132–3
    strategy level 148
    synergy 132
Business unit (defined) 139

C

Career paths
    base salary inversions 63, 102
    new ventures 165–6
    sales forces 56
    technical organizations 55
CBS 13
Churchill, Winston S. 148
Communication 3, 13, 29,
    103–4, 121, 124, 138, 201,
    203
Compensation mix 57, 62–3, 99,
    100–03, 106, 114–5
Compensation mix (defined) 45
Compensation objectives 31,
    161, 189

behavioral purposes 103
capital accumulation 8–9, 189, 191
financial leverage purposes 103
provincialism 153
recognition 15, 102, 192
Compensation objectives (defined) 39
Compensation policy wheel 24
Compensation surveys 24, 46, 50, 60–1, 101–3, 190–4
benchmark jobs 50
Business Week 5, 22
competitive pay 38–9, 50
labor pool shortages 49
long-term compensation survey data 190–4
annual compensation survey data 38, 39
Conformity 23
Consultants 5, 34, 77, 79, 84
executive search 38
Continental Illinois Bank 14, 130
Core objectives 182–4
Crystal, Graef S. 72–3

D
Decision making behavior 33, 40
decision processes 25, 105–6, 192–3
decision trade-offs 121
initiative 33, 39–40, 103–6, 108, 112–3, 147, 204
low-risk cultures 105
mission accountability networks (defined) 103

Deferral of payments 14–5
Discretionary awards 15
Distribution companies 126
Drucker, Peter F. 3, 56
Dupont (synthetic fiber division) 47

E
Eligibility criteria (for incentive pay)
base salary school 74
bonus eligibility 40, 103
hybrid performance units 78–83
long-term incentives 193–4
miscible school 74
new venture managers 163–7
nonmanagerial 55, 156, 162–3
organization level school 74
"outliers" 83–4, 161–2
salary grade school 73
staff jobs 25, 66, 160–2
vertical performance units 77–8
work cells 75, 78
Employee classes
bonus participation criteria (see eligibility criteria)
"castes" 13
organization hierarchy 40, 71
"outliers" 161–2
performance units 147, 153–60
performance units (defined) 17, 72
position taxonomy 26, 40
reporting level 4, 25, 71, 73–4, 102, 113, 117
Equity and equality 155–6

F

Financial measures
  earnings 12, 14, 120, 124,
    126, 136–9, 191
  gross revenues 126–7
  growth 14, 30, 82, 106,
    108–9, 127–8, 136–9, 156–
    7, 184–7
  quality of sales 127
  return 124, 128, 130, 133,
    136–9, 185–7
  sales (see also gross revenues)
    164, 167, 181
  short-term focus 20
Fireman, Paul 22, 101
Ford Motor Company 79
Functional measures
  administration 131
  finance 130
  manufacturing/operations 130
  marketing 129, 181
  qualification criteria 143–4

G

Gainsharing programs 29,
    141–3, 162–3
  Improshare 143
  Scanlon plan 141, 143
Geneen, Harold 52
General Electric 151
General Motors 11–3, 22, 47
Goldwyn, Sam 38

H

Henderson, Bruce 146
  Boston Consulting Group 85,
    144, 146, 151
Herman Miller, Inc. 108
Hewitt Associates 99

Holding companies 52, 121–2
Honeywell, Inc. 79

I

Iacocca, Lee 22
Improshare 143
Incentive compensation (defined)
    40, 59
Incentive objectives
  balancing the priorities 178
  composite performance profile
    121–2, 178–81
  core objective 182–4
  end results 41, 125
Internal equity 3–4, 45, 59, 62,
    117, 204

J

Jensen, Michael C. 5
Job evaluation 4, 48, 51, 54–6,
    106

K

Kelley, Robert 15

L

Labor markets 49–50
Leadership style 4, 12, 17, 39,
    167, 195, 197, 199–201
Long-term incentives
  book value stock purchase 199
  eligibility criteria 193–4
  restricted stock 30, 198
  shadow stock 195–6, 198
  stock options 30, 32, 189–91,
    198
  stock valuation formula 198
  strategic performance 195–6,
    200

thinly traded stock 199
Lump sum bonus 15

M
Management by objectives 74
Mandatory stock purchase 194
Matrix organization 78–9
McKinsey & Co. 85, 151
Meeting expectations perform-
    ance range 66–7
Middle management 12, 124–5,
    153
Murphy, Kevin J. 5

N
NASA 78–9
Neikirk, William 16
New venture managers 163–7
New ventures
    new venture careers 165–6
    stand-alone market value
        164–5

O
Organization analysis 77, 103
Organization development
    models 16–7
Orwell, George 37
"Outliers" (defined) 156
Ownership 12, 20, 189, 194,
    198–9

P
Payable performance range
    156–8
Payable performance range (de-
    fined) 148
Payment timing
    deferred compensation 32

employee loyalty 31, 32
    overlapping cycles 32
    vesting 32
Payout structure
    anguine schedule 170–6
    below target payouts 170–4
    compound incentives 181–5
    incentive weighting 185–7
    linear payout formula 169–70
    maximum payout 184
    payout grid 185–7
    payout schedule 42, 58, 123,
        158, 169–79
    payout threshold 171–4
    planning integrity 173–4
    probability distribution 170–1
    simplicity 4, 30, 52, 77,
        120–5
    zones 174–6, 185
Performance measure mix 158–9
Performance measures
    business portfolio enhance-
        ment 137
    business unit 139–41
    composite performance profile
        121–2
    corporate 135–9
    distribution companies 126
    ease of communication 138,
        141
    evaluation criteria 133–6
    functional area 142–3
    independence from capital
        structure 137
    long-term stockholder value
        137
    management's value added 12,
        40

NOPAT (net operating profits after taxes) 138
peer group comparability 137–8
performance management hypotheses 86–97
programmatic goals 176–81
performance scenarios 122–4
short-term stockholder return 136, 138
uncertainties in objective setting 6, 78
Performance range (defined) 148
Performance (defined) 40–1
Peters & Waterman
In Search of Excellence 22, 153
Porter, Michael E.
Competitive Strategy
Pratt, Edmund S. 6
Private companies 15, 189
Product shares 82
Productivity incentives 8
Profit sharing 8, 12, 15, 21–3, 28, 47, 126
Programmatic objectives (see also functional measures)
qualification criteria 143–4

R
Red circling 48–9, 51
Reebok
Fireman, Paul 22, 101

S
Salary increases
COLA (cost of living adjustments) 46
cost control 38, 47
demotions 49

lump sum merit bonuses (see also lump sum bonus) 47–8
merit increases 46–8, 62–3, 67–8
pay freeze 49
red circling 46–50
sliding scale 47
Salary reductions 68–70
Salary structures
benefits integration 63–5
dual career ladder 55
sales force 54–7
shop floor personnel 56
technical organizations 55
total compensation 42, 45, 57–70, 73, 83
work cell organizations 56
Sales forces 8, 28–9, 32, 43, 54–7
Scanlon plan 141, 143
Securities Industry Association 17
Shadow stock 195–6, 198
Simplicity 4–5, 30, 52, 77, 104, 120–5
Sloan, Alfred 12, 15
Smith, Adam
Paper Money 44
Steelcase, Inc. 108
Stock appreciation rights 195–6
Stock options 189–91
Stock ownership (see also ownership)
"mandatory" stock purchase 194
Strategic compensation milestones 143–4
Strategic performance 196, 200
Strategy models 148–53

growth/share matrix 148,
   151–3
product life cycle 148–51
strategy levels 132–3, 139–41

T
Target limit (defined) 66–7
Target performance 42, 66, 171
   objectives 74
   planning precision 41, 158,
      171
   practical performance range
      28, 182
Target performance (defined)
   28, 41–2
Tax effectiveness
   1986 Tax Reform Act 7, 190
   capital gains tax 7, 16, 189–90
Taylor, Frederick W. 78
Triad 34, 35

Twain, Mark 101

U
United Airlines 11

V
Vesting schedule 32

W
Walt Disney Company
   Eisner 21–2
Weighting of performance
   measures 148, 156, 158–60
Windfalls 28, 176, 184
Work force knowledge 3

Y
Yankelovich, Daniel
   McNamara Fallacy 161